Rhino Revolution

Rhino Revolution

Searching for new solutions

Clive & Anton Walker

JACANA

PREVIOUS SPREAD: A pair of black rhino cool off in a waterhole in Etosha National Park. Photo: Michael Viljoen.

OPPOSITE: Dr Anthony Hall-Martin. Photo: REF Archive.

FOLLOWING SPREAD: Visitors to the desert regions of Namibia viewing a rare desert rhino. Photo: Wilderness Safaris/Dana Allen.

First published by Jacana Media
(Pty) Ltd in 2017

10 Orange Street
Sunnyside
Auckland Park 2092
South Africa
+2711 628 3200
www.jacana.co.za

© Clive and Anton Walker, 2017

All artwork © Clive Walker

All rights reserved.

ISBN 978-1-4314-2568-6

Cover design and layout by Shawn Paikin
Set in Goudy 10.5/15pt
Printed and bound by Imago
Job no. 003114

See a complete list of Jacana titles
at www.jacana.co.za

Note: The opinions expressed by third parties or quotes in this publication are not necessarily those of ours.

In memory of
Anthony Hall-Martin

This book is dedicated to the late Dr Anthony Hall-Martin, who passed away in 2014. He was a long-time colleague and close friend of Clive's for 40 years. Anthony, possibly more than anyone, deserves our praise for his pioneering efforts in expanding the country's national park system and for his dogged determination to bring back the subspecies *Diceros bicornis bicornis* that once abounded from Namibia down into the western and northern Cape.

Anthony was not only a champion of the black rhino, he was also passionate about them. You can read more about this amazing individual in the book *Baobab Trails*. He set an amazing example, which is hard to duplicate, and if he were alive today, he would be a co-author of this book.

In the wider world of conservation, Anthony will be remembered and acknowledged for his distinguished career as a wildlife biologist, researcher and as a decision-taking senior executive, firstly with SANParks with whom he spent 25 years (14 as director), and then as a consultant specialising in biodiversity conservation throughout Africa, endangered species management and the private sector management of protected areas (Africa Parks).
– Lynn Hurry, October 2014

Contents

OPPOSITE: A female black rhino and her calf. Photo: Wilderness Safaris/Dana Allen.

Preface

The lack of spiritual space for the rhinos in local and international cultures has contributed more than a little to its endangerment. Endowed with no godly significance and no usefulness during life, rhinos are objectified commodities. The problem of the international conservation movement then is to give people a reason to keep rhinos around. Rhino conservation struggles to cast this odd animal in a new iconography. Conservation of wild animals relies upon the creation of new meanings – some might even say new mythologies – with global appeal. Media attention on the unsteady fate of rhinoceroses often argues for the end of poaching by laying out graphic images of rhino slaughter. Instead of appealing to audiences with scenes of aesthetically pleasing rhino, or attempting to make rhinos cute, conservationists expose human brutality. Piles of disembodied horns suggest unstoppable greed. By saving the rhinoceros, they argue, we are saving ourselves from our own brutal nature and savage greed. Does the continued existence of rhinos serve only to prove our own mortality? While there are ecological reasons for maintaining the diversity of life on Earth, most conservation literature calls upon sympathy to motivate the masses. The state of wildlife conservation has reached a precipitous point for many species. It is a frightening fact that the future existence of rhinoceroses is entirely dependent upon the will of humans. Rhinos must find another way to carry their fortune – off their noses.

– Kelly Enright, 2008

FOLLOWING SPREAD: A lone black rhino against the backdrop of the Kunene region mountains in northern Namibia. Photo: Wilderness Safaris/Dana Allen.

Introduction

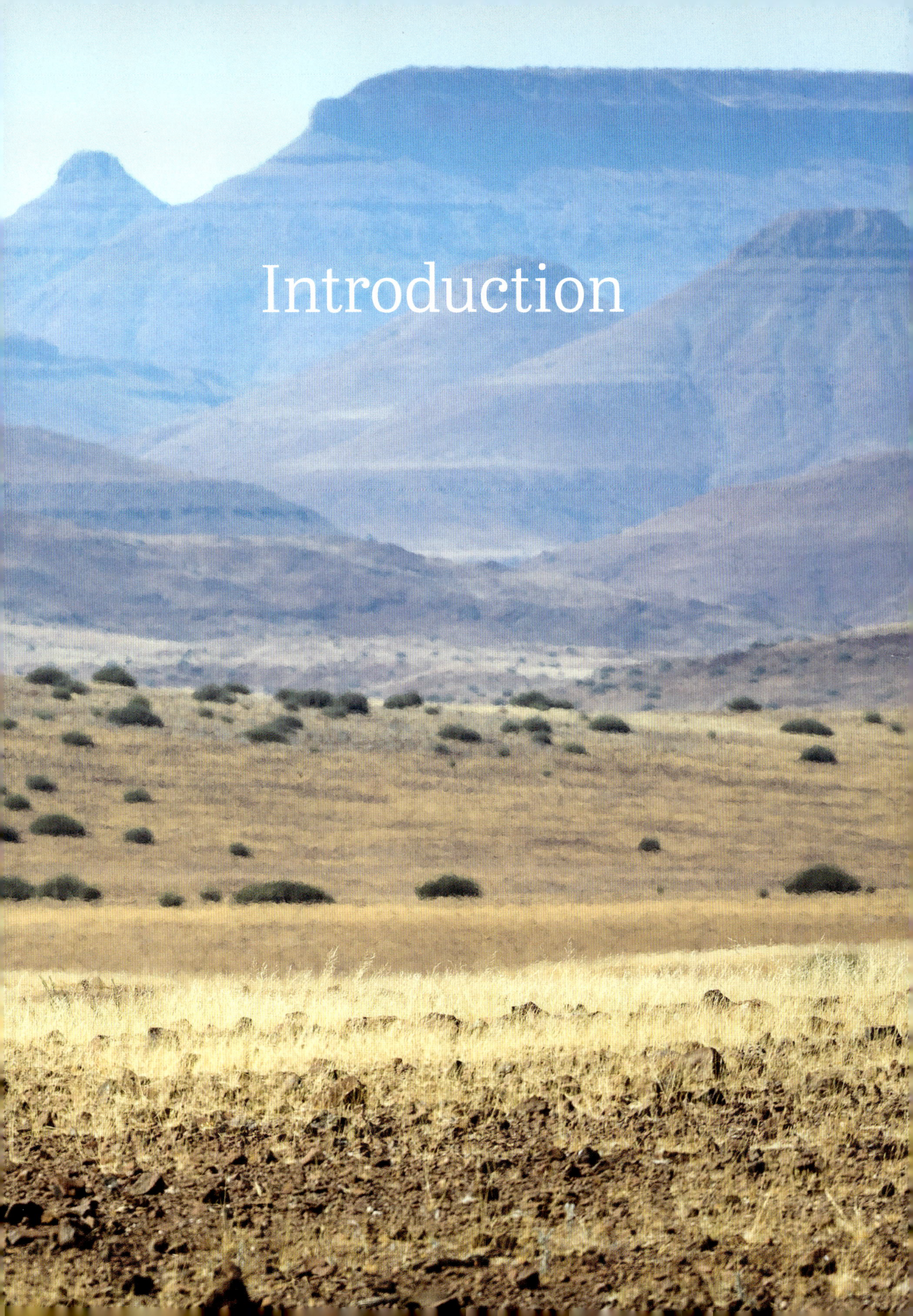

O Fortune / Like the moon
Ever changing
Rising first then declining

Dread destiny
And empty fate
An ever turning wheel
Who make adversity
And fickle health
Alike turning to nothing

In the dark
And secretly
You work against me
How through your trickery
My naked back
Is turned to you unarmed

Once on Fortune's throne
I sat exalted
Crowned with a wreath
Of prosperity's flowers
But from my happy
Flower-decked paradise
I was struck down
And stripped of all my glory

I lament the wounds that Fortune deals
With tear-filled eyes
For turning to the attack
She takes her gifts from me

Good fortune
And strength
Now are turned from me
Affliction
And defeat
Are always on duty
Come now
Pluck the strings
Without delay
And since by fate
The strong are overthrown
Weep ye all with me

– 12th Century poem

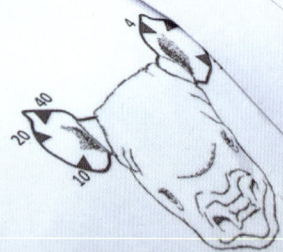

Counting the cost

This book sets out to illustrate the sheer power and beauty of rhino and the magnificence of the landscapes that are to be found in the encouraging conservation work being undertaken. Furthermore, it is the opinion of the authors and many colleagues involved in rhino conservation that the battle for the rhino is far from over, and while statistics would appear to indicate otherwise, all is not lost by any means. Yes, everyone is exhausted and horrified by events over the past 10 years and there are reasons for this as illustrated in the text; however, we have come to realise that we have to shift focus rapidly and this is occurring as we speak ... although the war has yet to be won.

Some of the issues and questions discussed in the book are:
- What is happening today to both species of African rhino in South Africa?
- What lessons have we learnt from the past, if any?
- What aspects of human transformation of the landscape have there been since 1994?
- What is the future of this iconic species?
- Will a legal trade in rhino horn help or harm the rhino's chances of survival?

Rhino Revolution is largely a sequel to *Rhino Keepers*, published in 2012 by Jacana Media and now out of print. We have included the work of two contributors, namely the late Jim Feely, Chapter 6, and Sue Downie and Lucky Mavrandonis, Chapter 5. There is a great deal of scientific and technical literature devoted to the 'rhinoceros' – far more than you may imagine – and we certainly do not wish to add to this already well-researched body of work. However, the rhinoceros, and in particular the black rhino, has not enjoyed the popularity that lions or elephants have, and therefore most of the work has largely been limited to a scientific level.

This book would not have been possible without the extraordinary assistance rendered by those people mentioned in the acknowledgements. We are extremely grateful to all of them.

OPPOSITE: A Wilderness Safaris rhino monitor recording white rhino observations in the Okavango Delta. Photo: Wilderness Safaris/Dana Allen.

PREVIOUS SPREAD: A stunning image of a pair of black rhino in Kenya's Amboseli National Park prior to the slaughter of the park's rhino in the 1970s. Photo: Legendary Africa/Mohamed Amin/Peter Joffe.

A legally hunted trophy black rhino in a controlled hunting area of Zamibia in the 1950s.
Photo: Hans Bufe.

The journey to find the rhino begins

My search for the black rhino began in 1956 in the library of Hans Bufe, mentor and friend, while looking at photographs of hunting expeditions in the Luangwa Valley Game Reserve in what was then Northern Rhodesia (now Zambia).

The photograph in the library depicted a trophy-hunted black rhino with a game scout standing smartly to attention behind the fallen animal. Hans Bufe, an accomplished big game hunter, was of German descent and had accompanied an Austrian Count on safari as companion and interpreter on a legal rhino hunt on one occasion, the licence costing £100! Where they were hunting, black rhinos were common.

TOP: Black rhino bull photographed by the author in the Regents Park Zoo, London, in 1959.

BOTTOM: The author Clive Walker at 'Poachers Lookout' in Tsavo National Park, Kenya, in 1960. Photo: Angela Wigley.

*Little did they know that the species was to be
driven to extinction in that very valley and
throughout Zambia in the years to come.*

My second encounter with a black rhino was in the zoological gardens at Regents
Park in London in 1959 when I met a very sad-looking black rhino who I have no
doubt once roamed the Kenyan bush. My photograph reveals his misery.

The third encounter was in Kenya's Tsavo National Park in 1960, at the time
home to no less than 9 000 black rhino. From, ironically, 'Poachers Lookout' we
counted 10 rhino either lying down or standing in the shade of thorn trees against
the backdrop of Mount Kilimanjaro. The horror of that lookout name was to prove
prophetic, as poachers in time succeeded in killing every rhino in that park, as
well as slaughtering thousands of elephants. Tsavo is Kenya's largest park at around
20 800 km^2 and was once home to not only thousands of black rhino but tens of
thousands of elephants too. Situated between Nairobi and Mombasa on the coast,
the park is divided into east and west, separated by the main road and railway line.
Never did I ever imagine that my destiny would be linked to the black rhino. I
knew absolutely nothing about there being at least five subspecies occupying 22 sub-
Saharan countries from the west coast of Africa to Somalia in the east, and all the
way south to the dense bushveld of Zululand's Hluhluwe Game Reserve where the
last of the 19th-century slaughter had restricted them.

From that time on, I began to take more than a passing interest in the plight
of the black rhino after having met members of the then Natal Parks Board field
staff. In 1973 I founded the Endangered Wildlife Trust (EWT) with the assistance of
James Clarke, a highly respected journalist with the Johannesburg-based newspaper
The Star, and a friend, Neville Anderson. We were concerned about a number of
endangered species in southern Africa, which included the black rhino.

In 1980, I returned to Tsavo for an IUCN (International Union for the
Conservation of Nature) African rhino and elephant group meeting. As well as being
the Director of EWT, I was also a member of the African Elephant Specialist Group.
The population of the black rhino throughout Africa had plunged and suddenly
everyone was very concerned. I travelled to Kenya with Dr Anthony Hall-Martin,
also a member of the group, occupying both a role as elephant and rhino specialist.
In those days both groups held simultaneous meetings in different African venues.
Anthony and I had obtained special clearance to visit Kenya, as South Africans were
not welcome in most African countries due to our government's apartheid policies of
the time. Apart from us, there were two other South Africans – Dr Jeremy Anderson
and Peter Hitchins.

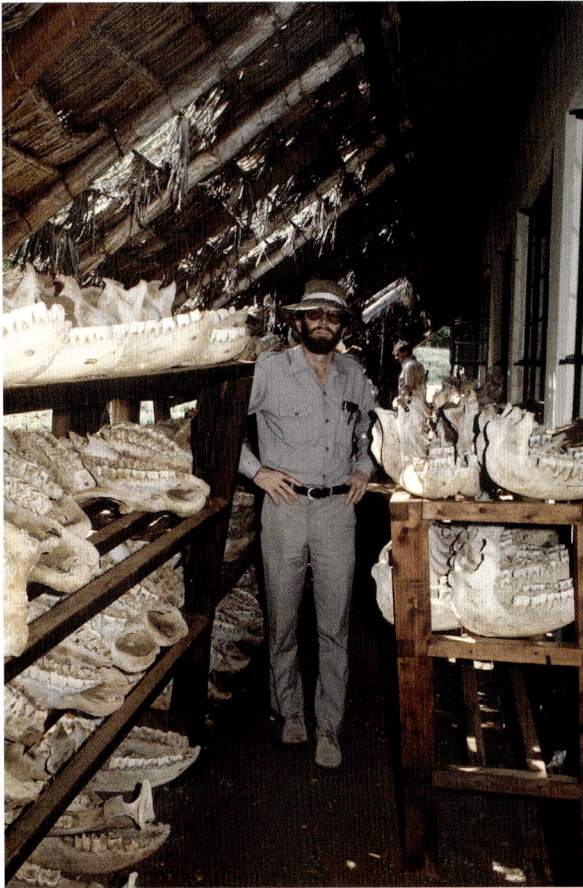

Dr Hall-Martin in the black rhino skull shed of Tsavo National Park in 1980. Photo: Clive Walker.

By the time of this second Tsavo visit, I had already come face to face with both the black and white rhino in Zululand while on wilderness trails. Peter Hitchins was at the time employed by the board and one of the very few people calling attention to the species he had been studying for the past 12 years in Hluhluwe Game Reserve. At the time, few were enthusiastic about the animal. Peter was to awaken in me a deep sense of awe of an animal that had a very bad and an equally misunderstood reputation.

In 1988 Anthony, Jeremy, Peter and I formed the Rhino and Elephant Foundation (REF). We have all remained committed and in contact ever since – apart from Anthony who sadly passed away in 2014.

For the last 44 years, the Walker family has been swept up with the world of both species of Africa's rhino – the work of EWT and the REF playing significant roles – and particularly with the founding and establishment of Lapalala Wilderness in the Waterberg of Limpopo (which was to become the first-ever, private black rhino sanctuary in South Africa in 1990). In 1985, my wife Conita and I, with the help of Dale Parker, owner of Lapalala Wilderness, established an environmental school where tens of thousands of school children, teachers and university students could meet the black rhino, Bwana, that lived in our garden. Karen Trendler, an expert animal rehabilitator, had raised Bwana first hand. He had been abandoned at birth and his care was taken over by Conita when he was six months old, raising him successfully to adulthood.

The first-ever museum dedicated to the five extant species, RHINO, was opened in 1989 in what was an old, abandoned 'farm school'. It was closed in 2007 due to a land claim and re-established 25 km away in 2017, the first and only one in South Africa. Bwana, the black rhino, was to become South Africa's first RHINO ambassador, followed by a white rhino calf, a hippopotamus and then a female black rhino calf, named Moêng, who was brutally slain in 2008 by poachers at the age of four at the commencement of the current crisis.

Our youngest son Anton, who is co-author of this book, grew up at Lapalala Wilderness, which became his second home from the age of 13, home to both species of African rhino and some of the most spectacular rhino habitat in Africa. Anton represents that new generation of game ranger who has to be both a wildlife and security specialist, in effect a CEO, economist, human resource specialist, mechanic, pilot and diplomat in a world that has become torn apart by greed and corruption. The unsung heroes in this battle are the unknown and unseen men and women under the command of what were once called 'game wardens'. Their staff face the task of protecting and conserving Africa's rhino daily, often in hostile, difficult terrain, putting their lives on the line. This book is also dedicated to all of them, wherever they may be.

This journey has not been mine alone. Both Anton and I have been privileged to travel and work with some amazing people – scientists, game rangers, pilots, wildlife managers, guides, field rangers, journalists, artists, conservationists, government civil servants and ordinary members of civil society. Some are well-known personalities, many are famous, the majority unknown. They all share the same interest with the exception of three groups: the politicians who largely pay lip service to conservation; the 'poachers' who are dealers in death; and the faceless, international crime dealers who represent the millions of consumers of rhino horn, collectors and investors who know little about this extraordinary creature from a bygone age and may have no idea what it even looks like. No one at this stage can offer a silver bullet to the dilemma, but this book seeks to tell the story of these amazing creatures and why we believe they are worthy of our highest respect, protection and determined efforts to ensure their survival.

The mingled destiny of Africa's rhino

The story of the rhino in southern Africa has been a bloody one from the time of the arrival of the first Europeans in 1652 and continues to this day. The species has largely survived due to the farsighted and timeous interventions of individuals in the past who recognised that the rhino would not survive the 'hand of man' if action was not taken. The tsetse fly and malaria played an important part in South Africa in the survival of the last pocket of white rhino and perhaps less than a hundred black rhino in the wilderness of what was then known as Zululand in 1894. One black rhino female survived in the Kruger National Park as late as 1936.

With the exception of the remote desert regions of the Kaokoveld, Namibia, the rhino was extinct by the turn of the 19th century. Botswana did not fare any better, with occasional sightings in Ngamiland up to 1994 when it finally became extinct. Zimbabwe and Zambia fared far better and a great deal of that had to do with dedicated field men and the old ally, the tsetse fly. As we all know, that was to change very dramatically, with Zambia losing all their rhino in the 1980s; and very nearly the same happening in Zimbabwe. Mozambique has always been a bit of a mystery, a long, protracted bush war did not help, and most certainly the species did not survive very long in the southern part of the country into the 20th century. They did occur

A rare specimen of the extinct quagga *(Equus quagga quagga)*. Photo: Museum of Natural History, Leyden, Holland.

in low numbers in the north. In Malawi, the species was regarded as extinct.

Where are we today and what has been achieved since the beginning of the 20th century? Before the turn of the 19th century, South Africa witnessed the extinction of three large species of mammal: the quagga (*Equus quagga quagga*), the Cape lion (*Panthera leo melanochaitus*) and the blue buck (*Hippotragus leucophaeus*). We nearly added both species of rhino, the bontebok (*Damaliscus dorcas*) and the Cape mountain zebra (*Equus zebra zebra*).

By contrast, the conservation of southern Africa's wildlife during the 20th century has certainly had its ups and downs, and there have been many hard-fought battles, especially for rhino and elephant. Unfortunately for both, mankind has had a love affair for a very long time with both species for there is something they possess that he covets ... the horn of one and the teeth of the other.

The last decade of the 20th century saw the final acts in the saga of Africa's most threatened large mammal – the black rhino (*Diceros bicornis*). In the 1960s there were about 65 000 black rhino occurring in 22 countries. Within 20 years poaching wiped out thousands and numbers dropped to 15 000 by 1980. A scant 10 years later there were no more than 3 500 remaining in 12 countries and, despite the international trade bans, the demand for rhino horn was as strong as ever. By 1994 the continental population had plunged to 2 400 and remained barely viable in just four African countries: Kenya, Zimbabwe, Namibia and South Africa.

Most recent publications on the topic of 'rhinoceros' paint a harrowing outlook for both of Africa's rhino species as the poaching continues with no less than 5 940 animals killed (AfRSG, March 2016) over the past eight years. The number killed at the time of writing, March 2017 (for 2016 numbers) amounts to 1 054 killed, according to the Department of Environmental Affairs, bringing the total since 2008 to 6 994. Most of the killing concerns the white rhino. However, it also includes the critically endangered black rhino, a species that is far more demanding of attention than the white rhino.

Not unlike the story of both the tiger and the elephant (elephant numbers in Africa are down to less than 500 000), the rhino treads a very fine line between extinction and survival. Their destiny is in our hands.

We all know the clock is ticking – and once again it is 'five minutes to midnight' for the world's surviving rhino. The choice is ours; once gone, they are gone forever.

After careful management and protection, South Africa slowly built up the southern subspecies of black rhino, *Diceros bicornis minor*, with introductions into the Kruger National Park from Zimbabwe and the then Natal Parks Board reserves, Hluhluwe

The author Clive Walker in his studio at Lapalala with two paintings of rhino. The one on the right is illustrated on page 10. Photo: Walker Archive.

and Imfolozi, in the '60s. The Kruger National Park became the most important haven for the black rhino outside of Zululand (as it was known before 1994) and, with its two million hectares, it had the benefit of habitat, space and sound management.

Today, more than ever, the dynamics have changed dramatically. We are fighting 'fire with fire', and for those human-rights activists out there who criticise the fact that 'people' too are dying in this conflict, they need to understand this is a 'war'. Poachers entering game reserves with the intention of killing rhino are in the main by no stretch of the imagination only starving peasants. Many are experienced former militia who are well armed and ruthless. They know the odds and they know the rewards. This is no longer 1994. If every available resource (be it drones, sniffer and tracker dogs, night-vision equipment, stun grenades, sophisticated automatic weapons and military trained officers) is deployed to counter them in this battle, it is but one element in the fight to save the rhino. Killing poachers alone won't win the war and we all recognise that.

We need a new philosophy in our approach to rhino survival. The South African landscape has changed dramatically. Human population expansion, immigration, crime, a bloated government civil service where corruption is considered 'sclerotic', incompetency in many areas of state enterprises, coupled with an enormous widening gap between the rich and poor, the perception that conservation is the pursuit of the rich and privileged persists ('Are rhinos more important than people').

Do not for one moment think that the rhino crisis of today is a repeat of what has gone before. The situation has changed dramatically with the escalation in the price of rhino horn in China and Vietnam for one thing – rhino horn today being worth more than gold. The dynamics have changed and so too have the international criminal syndicates where environmental crime ranks alongside that of drugs, arms, human trafficking and diamonds. The criminal justice system in South Africa appears woefully out of step and incapable of dealing forcefully with a system that is just way ahead of them. It is further questionable about how really committed the government is in even attempting to deal with the crisis at the highest level. As a consequence, we have lost credibility when it comes to environmental crime, and it is not unreasonable to question whether South Africa will ever really confront China head-on given their ever-increasing, cosy relationship. A government that does not even honour its own constitution is of great concern.

Under these circumstances, how do we engage 'communities' living alongside wildlife areas and bring them on board as meaningful role players and not as passive by-standers? This is a critical issue – in this book we explore examples where this is bringing about meaningful change.

It is time that a more positive note is introduced into the conversation which to date has largely centred around depressing poaching issues, statistics and those faceless individuals who drive the illegal trade and those who believe a legal trade is the answer.

Do not be fooled into believing there is an easy solution. Twenty years ago a poacher could expect to earn US$100–350 per pair of horns. Today the poacher is prepared to pay US$1 000 per night for a 'safe' house, let alone what the dealer is prepared to pay per kilogram of horn. The economic dynamics have changed dramatically – South Africa's unemployment stands at 8.3 million and rising, and that figure represents an awful lot of hungry people.

In spite of all these hurdles, there is excellent work that has quietly gone on in terms of range expansion of the species both at a state level and at the level of the increasing role being played by the private 'rhino keeper' within southern Africa. Many of these populations occur in diverse and spectacular landscapes, under sound management with programmes involving communities with strong tourism developments. All these areas are worthy of our attention and they are calmly getting on with these challenges. Dare I say we are optimistic about the rhino? The answer is, simply, yes we are. We have seen the results, and the dedication and commitment are there.

The stakes are high, very high; perhaps no other living creature has such a price tag on its head today.

Just how far have we come since the last rhino war?

This book endeavours to explore the reasons why South Africa finds itself today embroiled in the struggle to save the rhino. A war that started way back in a distant land in the '70s. There is no easy answer in a continent bedevilled by poverty, corruption and greed.

Today South Africa finds itself in a situation where the enemy is in its own backyard. It is so easy to lay the blame elsewhere beyond our own shores. We are in fact fighting two battles: the battle on the ground, which is costly, dangerous and problematic in terms of sustainability; and a second more insidious one within South Africa at a state level, which appears to be in terminal decline linked to the socio-economic situation prevailing today. Even with the finest fighting force on the ground in the struggle, if the levers of power in high office don't function or don't care, the ongoing war will be a bloody one. There is, however, some hope, for South Africa is unique in that it has a citizenry that has shown it can stand alone at great cost and dedication and this provides the hope for the rhinoceros. All those concerned and committed folk out there who have supported and continue to support the battle to save the rhino deserve our utmost admiration.

In the case of the rhino in Africa, the problem is not entirely of our making in spite of all our own faults ... it lies elsewhere. As long as the belief exists, and it has done so for a very long time, that the horns they carry on the top of the nose are essential to good health and wellbeing, somewhere, far away in another place someone is going to seek them.

We have made every effort to ensure that the facts and other information are accurate in this work. In a complex and somewhat overcrowded world of so many voicing their opinions on how to save the rhino, the subject is sensitive and understandably very emotional. We recognise and respect this, but one question we are unable to answer is the question of 'trust'. There appears to be a high level of mistrust prevailing in South African society today. This does not help in any way when, as explained by Kelly Enright in the Preface, 'the future existence of the rhinos is entirely dependent on the will of humans'.

FOLLOWING SPREAD: A magnificent female white rhino and newborn calf. Photo: WRSA/ Quintus Strauss.

CHAPTER 1

Rhino wars – guns and rhinos go together

I do not see how the rhinoceros can be permanently preserved, save in very out-of-the-way places or in regular reserves.

– President Theodore Roosevelt

A far-sighted vision

In his book *African Game Trails*, former president Theodore Roosevelt's fears proved disastrously true when the northern subspecies of the white rhino was declared extinct in the wild by 2010.

What he omitted to add was the number he and his son Kermit killed on his prolonged safari, long planned by his big-game-hunting friend, Fredrick Courtney Selous, of the very species that is now extinct. They killed a total of nine rhino, which was well over the permitted limit – excessive by any standards and more so given their scarce standing even at that time.

It is noteworthy that as a politician Roosevelt nonetheless stands head and shoulders above most for his far-sighted vision and action in declaring reserves and national parks in the USA during his presidency. He set an example that ushered in a new era of conservation of protected areas across the world, not least in Africa.

Joining the fight to save the Zambian and Zimbabwean rhinos

Historically, Zambia had an enormous number of black rhino, found mainly in the Luangwa basin of south-east Zambia. South Luangwa, North Luangwa and Lukusuki were proclaimed as game reserves in 1938. The recommendations were made by Captain Pitman, who was chief game warden in Uganda in 1931 and had been seconded to Northern Rhodesia (Zambia). He clearly saw the areas had enormous value, especially with the presence of large numbers of black rhino, and he produced a comprehensive and far-sighted report suggesting the establishment of a number of reserves and the setting up of an elephant control department.

Among those early men employed to control elephant was Norman Carr, appointed in 1939. Norman was joined by Bertie Schultz and they were the only two senior men in this entire region at that time. Norman went off to fight in World War II in 1940 and upon his return he rejoined the department, finally retiring in 1961. He then went on to establish the first hunting operation and first-ever walking safaris in Africa.

OPPOSITE: A white rhino in the early morning expels vapour from its wide nostrils as it faces the photographer. Photo: WRSA/Meldt van der Spuy.

PREVIOUS SPREAD: The awesome Zambezi river viewed from the Zimbabwean side. Poachers from Zambia would have to risk crossing this river in dugout canoes to poach rhino in Zimbabwe. Photo: Clive Walker.

LEFT: A Zimbabwean parks ranger prepares to exit a makeshift boma as the black rhino starts to react from an immobilising drug. Photo: REF Archive/Glen Tatham.

RIGHT: Zimbabwe did not have the luxury of modern equipment, so rangers had to do the heavy lifting in capture operations in the race to save rhino. Photo: REF Archive/Glen Tatham.

Norman became something of a legend in his lifetime and together with his colleagues established an area of 63 000 km², which by 1972 had been proclaimed a national park. At the time of proclamation, it had an estimated population of 100 000 elephant and over 12 000 black rhino. In 1962, we met for dinner at the Courtfield Gardens Hotel, London, where he was staying (I was the assistant manager of the Courtfield Gardens Hotel group at the time). Norman was in London to promote a book he had written on the rearing of two lions, Big Boy and Little Boy. My interest in Norman was the fact that he knew my mentor, Hans Bufe, who was a frequent elephant hunter in the Luangwa Valley in the '50s. Another of my mentors was Jim Feely, who in 1962 was employed in elephant control in the same area (Jim has written the chapter 'Black rhino, white rhino – what's in a name?').

By 1984 the Luangwa Valley was embroiled in massive poaching of rhino and elephant from within the country. The situation was so bad that Norman Carr and others concerned with the area had initiated the formation of an anti-poaching unit, Save the Rhino Trust, to assist government in combatting the problem. The trust did incredible work with support from various international conservation organisations, and enormous funds raised by well-meaning people; but in spite of their best efforts, they could not stem the tide of poaching. In the end the poachers killed them all ... Zambia lost every single rhino.

While Zambia's rhinos were dwindling and difficult to locate, the stage was set for the poachers to move across the Zambezi River into the well-stocked parks of Zimbabwe. Here similar efforts were being made to halt the poaching. Glen Tatham was the commander of what became Operation Stronghold in Zimbabwe's effort to prevent this back in 1984. He and his men knew they were up against a very determined foe who were not prepared to lay down their weapons when called upon to do so; firing first, killing park's staff and being killed themselves in turn.

In that country they don't talk about patrolling parks ...
they talk war; they talk about counter-insurgency;
and they go out with machine guns.

In 1985 the Wildlife Society of Zimbabwe and the Zambezi Society, with massive public support and promotion, had raised funds for much-needed field equipment: tents, mosquito nets, backpacks, water bottles and sleeping bags. The International NGO community had also rallied. Notable among them were two American friends of ours, Babette Alferie and Ingrid Schroeder of SAVE US. Their support was crucial, as was that of the World Wide Fund for Nature (WWF). Later, in 1986, the newly formed Rhino and Elephant Foundation likewise stepped up in providing spare parts for vehicles, radios, backpacks and tents. Every bit of support made a difference and Zimbabwe's rhino survival campaign became a familiar voice on T-shirts and in the media.

In March of 1985 the right of park staff to use their weapons against poachers was given by the Zimbabwean Ministry of Home Affairs. This shoot-to-kill policy was at first met with a good deal of condemnation and controversy from abroad. As so often is the case, Africa gets told by the West what is best for it, most often by well-meaning but misguided people who sit so far away from the situation as to be utterly blind to the forces at work on the ground.

What is really frustrating is that the real enemy is invisible. Who are these faceless, grey men who move between the world's capitals? They take little risk compared to the poacher who, in those days, received a pittance. The blood of 3 000 black rhino was to soak into Zimbabwe's soil with the blood of at least 180 poachers alongside them, as well as the blood of park rangers. The killing of poachers was not a deterrent in itself, but you cannot expect men or woman to defend a valuable animal, such as rhino and elephant, armed only with radios and antiquated .303s. The mere presence of well-armed rangers sends a clear signal that you mean business, but in itself is not the means to an end; one requires all the necessary back up and support.

Governments have either been powerless to intervene or, as has been the case in some instances, elements within government have been complicit themselves. The same scenario was repeating itself – from Uganda down, the spiral working ever-increasingly south. South Africa had virtually seen all its rhino wiped out by the turn of the 19th century, but had managed to recover. It now had only Zimbabwe between it and Zambia. If Zimbabwe was to follow Zambia, would South Africa be next? We will deal more fully with questions surrounding the funding needed to protect rhino in Chapter 4 as it is very relevant to what has befallen South Africa since 2008.

South Africa had had sufficient warning and was fully aware of what had transpired in the rest of Africa. We were slowly waking up to the fact that we had to seriously review our plans and policies and consider what needed to be done to protect ourselves from this looming threat.

OPPOSITE TOP AND BOTTOM: A black rhino at Mana Pools National Park. The majority of the park's rhino population was largely wiped out by Zambian poachers. Photos: Torre Balance.

The 1984 Pilanesberg Rhino Workshop

In September of 1983, Peter Hitchins and I accompanied Anthony Hall-Martin to four of the National Parks Board's parks on a fact-finding mission to assess suitability of the areas for the reintroduction of the black rhino, visiting Vaalbos (to the west of Kimberley), Augrabies Falls, the Karoo and the Mountain Zebra Park. All of these were judged to be most suitable. Unfortunately the Augrabies Falls National Park was later to become the subject of a land claim and the rhino had to be moved to the other chosen reserves.

The original Cape rhino (*Diceros bicornis bicornis*) is the nominate subspecies, but was regarded as being extinct (the last rhino in the Cape being shot near Addo in 1852). Yet others were convinced that the black rhino of Damaraland and Kaokoland belong to the same taxon. As the Namibian rhino are geographically the closest to the Cape rhino (the distribution of the black rhino was continuous from the Cape to Etosha), there was considerable merit in the suggestion, according to Hall-Martin. Today it is widely accepted on all grounds – ecologically, genetically and practically – as the logical choice for the founder stock of black rhino to be introduced to the arid zones of South Africa. For reasons of security, the parks are not identified. Chapter 5 (by L. Mavrandonis and S. Downie) well illustrates the success story of the return of this subspecies.

An APU (anti-poaching unit) operational base deep in the bush of a Zimbabwean National Park. Photo: REF Archive/Glen Tatham.

In February of the following year (1984), the first Rhino Workshop was convened by the Endangered Wildlife Trust (EWT) in Pilanesberg Game Reserve. It was attended by leading members of the then four provinces, the police, the Zoological Gardens of Johannesburg and Pretoria, South West Africa (Namibia), the National Parks Board of South Africa, Bophuthatswana (North West) and the IUCN Rhino Specialist Group. It was chaired by Peter Hitchins, and the primary aim was to increase the numbers and distribution of the black rhino in southern Africa – although a range of other factors were discussed as follows:

- Kruger National Park: good security and no rhino poached; the only problem was how does Kruger get more rhinos?
- Pilanesberg: no problems; effective control of the rhino populations.
- Transvaal: house in order; no poaching known.
- Natal: there had been only one serious poaching problem in 1981 (two black and two white rhino); the Natal reserves remained the principal source of both species of rhino in South Africa (for the state in the case of black rhino; and for the state and private sector in the case of white rhino).
- South West Africa: of considerable concern was the situation regarding the rhino of the Kaokoveld and their future; it was reported that poaching was no longer a problem; it was another source of rhino taking place first on government land and later on private land.

A captured Zambian poacher being interrogated by members of a Zimbabwean APU.
Photo: REF Archive/Glen Tatham.

Recovered rhino horn, elephant tusks, an axe, boots and AK-47 ammunition clips. Photo: REF Archive/Glen Tatham.

It is important to note how the situation within South Africa has changed since then: the development of a large number of private rhino owners of both black and white rhino up until 1990; the change in democracy after 1994 and the cessation of hostilities; the huge influx of illegals into South Africa; nine provinces as opposed to the original four; and the socio-economic-political factors.

To further illustrate the point, one needs to look at the totals of rhino for 1984, 2011 and 2016 in South Africa.[1]

- 1984: White rhino: 3 250   Black rhino: 610
- 2011: White rhino: 21 000   Black rhino: 4 881
- 2016: White rhino: 19 682–21 077   Black rhino: 5 042–5 455

In 1984 one of the key issues was the long-term distribution of both subspecies of black rhino. An important event took place 18 months later in July 1985 when six black rhino (subspecies *bicornis bicornis*) were returned to the Cape from South West Africa after an absence of 133 years – this was funded by EWT. Their destination was the Augrabies Falls National Park in the north-western Cape, and the re-establishment took place under the direction of Anthony Hall-Martin.

Establishment of the Rhino and Elephant Foundation (REF)

The idea to set up the REF first materialised on the back of a Land Rover in the desert of Namibia's Damaraland in 1984. I had just told Anthony Hall-Martin and Peter Hitchins that I planned to step down as director of the Endangered Wildlife Trust (EWT). Their concern sprang from the realisation that once I departed, there may no longer have been the same interest in rhino and elephant by those who would take over from me.

Peter felt very strongly that a major threat was on its way. What, he asked, if the threat was to prove true and there was possibly no organisation devoted to the species? Why not form an organisation with that particular brief to protect rhinos and elephants? I was less than enthusiastic as I had spent the past 12 years very involved in the EWT and my energies were being channelled into a new game reserve that had rhino; my interest in environmental education was also paramount.

By now Anthony had moved to Skukuza in the Kruger National Park and both species came under his watch; he clearly supported Peter in the need to establish an organisation devoted to protecting the future of both species of pachyderm. With all three of us being intensely interested in rhinos and elephants, it was inevitable that I would cave in and agree to form a group with these animals as its overriding concern. By 1986, despite our assorted other commitments, the prospect had really taken hold and we began working seriously towards forming a group of some kind. At first I pushed for it to be affiliated to the EWT as a working group because of my past connections with them, but Peter and Anthony felt it could constrain the group. Thus, the REF came into being, with Anthony assuming the role of first chairman.

It was predictable that there would be widespread dismay at yet another conservation movement encroaching on an already overloaded 'Ark'. Competition was unavoidable by virtue of the fact that one winds up competing for funds and for the backing of individuals and corporations. In this area the REF faced its most severe critics. I tried to overcome my concerns by assuring myself we had entered into a period of war against rhino in particular, and as a specialist organisation we could devote all our energy into the emerging struggle and not be side tracked by other conservation issues.

The REF was formally established in 1988. As a small new organisation, it was supported in a spectacular way by an impressive body of individuals who lent their names and support to the organisation. Dr Mangosuthu Buthelezi was the president, and Ian Player and David Shepherd were patrons, together with a number of prominent advisors from various countries who were highly experienced in the conservation of both species, such as Dr David Cumming from Zimbabwe, Dr Iain Douglas-Hamilton, the late Peter Jenkins from Kenya, Dr Jeremy Anderson, Dr Norman Owen-Smith (brother of Garth of Kaokoland fame and author of *An Arid Eden*), as well as my old friend Prof. Koos Bothma, all from South Africa. The support also included three Homeland Boards, the Natal Parks Board and the National Parks Board of South Africa. The organisation was unique in that it had exactly one paid staff member, Rozanne Savory, who was a living dynamo, handling every aspect from sticking stamps to fundraising.

The Boards brochure reflected the philosophy in the following words:

We live in a world where man has stretched out his hand to touch the stars, where he has left his mark upon the dark dim world of the ocean floors and where the most inhospitable parts of the Earth hold no fear for him. Experience has shown that sensible application of state and private funding can reverse the decline of rhino and elephant populations.

Something had to be done – and done very soon – for by now the war was on South Africa's very doorstep. There was not a moment to lose.

The 1988 Skukuza Rhino Workshop

With these words by the boards, the REF got off to a spectacular start by staging a Rhino Workshop in conjunction with the Game Rangers Association of Africa to be held at Skukuza in the Kruger National Park in 1988. It was to become a landmark event for it was attended by virtually everyone in the known rhino world, including politicians, law enforcement, scientists, game rangers, policy makers, conservationists, fundraisers, journalists and corporate supporters. We certainly had no qualms from whom we accepted funding.

The horror story of the wiping out of Africa's black rhino was spelt out at the workshop by experts from across the continent, as a sad tale of human avarice and greed leading to the virtual extinction of one of the Earth's largest and most magnificent land mammals. The rhino war had been raging for at least 10 years, starting in central Africa, and rolling down the east coast, through Uganda, Kenya and Tanzania, into Zambia and Zimbabwe, and was now about to spill over into South Africa. From a total population of 15 000 in 1980, Africa's black rhino numbered just 3 700 and that number was dropping rapidly.

On the one side of this war were the international crime syndicates – the organised crime rings, who were cashing in on the fortunes being made in supplying rhino horn to ready markets in the Middle East for the manufacture of dagger handles and in the Far East for traditional medicine; and ranged against this formidable foe were Africa's beleaguered game rangers and conservationists. At that point in time the latter was losing. Speakers were to reveal the various measures taken to halting the slaughter: using military strike units to seek out and destroy the poachers on the ground in Zimbabwe; providing armed guards for individual surviving rhino; getting the local population's support in Namibia; relocating rhino away from danger zones; placing rhino into intensive protection zones (IPZs); and a host of other issues.

The value of IPZs (small, enclosed sanctuaries) was that there was a higher concentration of rangers, improved surveillance and monitoring and a greater possibility of rhino-to-rhino contact.

Dr David Cumming summed up the workshop with a number of relevant points:

- In the past six years there has been a 70% decline in black rhino populations.
- 75% of the black rhino population groups remaining consist of less than 50 animals.
- We know very little about the dynamics of the rhino horn trade.
- There is a need for wildlife agencies to cooperate with other organisations, such as police and customs in all the countries involved.
- The answer may be to withdraw endangered populations to smaller areas where they can be better protected.
- Survey techniques need to be improved – many of the censuses are little better than educated guesses.
- Corrupt politicians have nullified the efforts of good conservation people and policies.
- Rhino conservation has not been put into the broader prospective of overall conservation.
- The militarist view of anti-poaching must be considered as a 'holding action' (fight back/shoot to kill in self-defence).
- There is a need to deal with the socio-economic realities of each country and bring in 'other' expertise to embed conservation in the very ethics of the country.
- The diversity of individuals is the greatest ally and force in conservation and with it must go the humility to communicate with all.

Glen Tatham, Commander of Operation Stronghold, Zimbabwe. Photo: REF Archive.

A number of important lessons were learnt at the workshop, not least the need to establish protection units, such as the Endangered Species Protection Unit of the South African Police, the African Rhino Owners Association and the Southern African Development Community (SADC – and their Rhino Management Group and security group), which was headed up by the late Nick Steele (formerly of the Natal Parks Board and later the KwaZulu Bureau of Natural Resources). Some aspects at the workshop were either ignored or the relevant budgets were not going to be forthcoming. This was critical and has been borne out today.

Other work in Africa at the time of the workshop indicated that there should be one man per 20 km^2 in the field with a recurrent annual expenditure of US$400 per km^2. That figure today is US$4 400 per 10 km^2. Nick Steele always maintained that the best way to keep poaching levels down was to have 'feet' on the ground – well-trained, well-equipped, dedicated, well-led men with the best backup possible. If you are reading this and you are a rhino owner or are responsible for rhino, have you ever taken his advice? There may, however, be factors that mitigate against this as you may have little or no control over budgets. This has been the problem in many state-run reserves and, as we believe today, is also true in most private rhino sanctuaries.

In an interview at the workshop, Glen Tatham, at the time Chief Warden for Zimbabwe's National Parks, said:

> It's a war: the Zambezi Valley, an area of some 12 000 km^2 bordering Zambia consists of some of the best wildlife country in Africa. An area of spectacular landscapes, stretching from the Kariba Gorge in the west travelling east and parallel to the mighty Zambezi River to the Chewore Hills in the east and home to an astonishing array of wildlife. The 'valley' comprises large areas of mopane scrub and acacia woodland interspersed by ancient baobab trees, and along the alluvial floodplains woodlands of ana trees (*Faidherbia albida*) and Natal mahogany (*Trichilia emitica*). This was the last line of defence for the black rhino, an animal that once covered most of central, eastern and southern Africa. Poachers have drastically reduced their numbers everywhere else. If they succeed here, that could be the end of the black rhino in the wild.

At the workshop, Glen Tatham and Russell Taylor advised the meeting that Zimbabwe still had an estimated 2 000 black rhino. The largest population of some 750 animals was located in the middle of the Zambezi Valley between Kariba and Kenyemba. By then the 'war of the rhino' had started in earnest, having got seriously underway in 1984, coinciding as it did with the decimation of Zambia's last rhino in the Luangwa Valley. From July of that year, poaching of rhino had intensified to an alarming degree by Zambian nationals crossing the river. They were serious and they meant business. They were armed with sophisticated weapons: AK-47s, Nato G3s, SKSs, .303s and .375 hunting rifles. Zimbabwe marshalled its efforts and fought back with the support of the Zimbabwe National Conservation Trust.

'Time is running out for our rhino; they don't get a chance to die of natural causes anymore,' we were to hear at the workshop. We learnt that Zimbabweans themselves had now entered the picture. Rhino poaching by Zimbabweans, which had remained at very low levels, had suddenly begun to escalate six months earlier. Zimbabwe's fight to save its rhino had entered a dark hour. In the words of a senior official:

I think you have got to accept that illegal hunting is increasing in Africa for the foreseeable future in a major way ... The emphasis should be on early detection. The state of affairs in Africa now is incredibly poor economic conditions, a breakdown of law and order, impoverished people who have no prospect of a reasonable living ... They are going to go for rhino wherever the opportunity crops up.

An important aspect coming out of the workshop was the opportunity to meet the many men who, not unlike Glen Tatham, lead the forces in the war against poachers; the men and women who don't go to wildlife conferences and rub shoulders with the 'big' names in wildlife, but whose job it is to be out on patrol in all kinds of weather, night and day. They are the front-line defence – and yet in the '80s and '90s, they earned dismal salaries, and largely still do in most of Africa. Sadly, most African governments do not commit enough funding when it comes to their wildlife estates, and particularly their staff. The evidence was there and in plain view of everyone. Without the outside support of national and international NGOs, the battle in countries like Kenya, Tanzania, Zimbabwe, Namibia and Botswana would have been that much more difficult and, as we all know, poaching continues to this very day.

The proposal surrounding the establishment of the Endangered Species Protection Unit (ESPU) was an important landmark decision taken at the workshop and it contributed immensely towards preventing the war spilling over into South Africa. One of the principal reasons why the ESPU was formed in 1989 was to combat the illegal trade, and this led to many interceptions and arrests of dealers and middlemen. The organisation under the leadership of Colonel Piet Lategan went on to achieve a high level of success, eventually operating with some 22 officers.

The 1988 Rhino Workshop brought everything to the fore and made it very plain as to what actions were necessary. The delegates had all been shocked about the black rhino and, as with so many of these meetings, more paper and talk was churned out to find ways to halt the killing, but the blood of rhino continued to stain the African veld.

The last stronghold of the rhino was in fact under siege.

Nearly 30 years have passed since that gathering took place in Skukuza, where some of the best minds in the world of rhino conservation were collected under one roof. We deal with the socio-economic question in Chapter 2, which reveals that, considering the militaristic view of anti-poaching as a holding action, this is unrealistic in today's climate in South Africa. By 'holding action' we mean fighting back or shooting to kill in self-defence. We were fighting fire with fire and the poacher of 1988 is far removed from the sophisticated poacher of today. The critical suggestion of withdrawing endangered populations to smaller areas did not at the time receive the attention it should have. We are now of the opinion that that is a vital option as large parks and reserves, while ideal from a biodiversity point of view, are chronically flawed when it comes to the economic reality of protecting rhino on the ground. It is simply not sustainable and does not make biodiversity sense. As we enter the ninth year of this rhino carnage, we are aware that this ongoing killing is hugely costly and is depriving other aspects of biodiversity conservation of its vitally needed funding.

The worst was yet to come

In an urgent bid to stop the poaching, Zimbabwe commenced an experimental dehorning programme of white rhino in 1991, and later the policy was adopted for black rhino. The programme, however, did not prove successful, especially in Hwange National Park where all the dehorned animals were slaughtered in any event. It is fair to say that it could have been worthwhile, but it would not achieve any success if all the other components were not in place: anti-poaching equipment, improved salaries and benefits to staff, and an increase in manpower. Sadly, the opposite happened and staff were retrenched in Zimbabwe. At the time, I wrote that unless governments make serious attempts to protect these assets and the men guarding them, we face a bleak future. There were times when my colleagues and I wondered if we weren't wasting our time. The sad saga across Africa was depressing … all the hype, the fundraising, the banners, the T-shirts, the media, the spears and insults thrown at us for daring to stick our heads above ground shouting 'enough is enough'. Who was listening to us? Whose rhino were they in any event?

Of course, it really *was* worthwhile, for that is what humanity should be about. Rhino don't belong to anyone, they belong to the world, and if we as humans cannot do anything to prevent their mindless extinction because of a belief by people halfway round the world who are convinced of the efficacy of rhino horn in traditional medicine, we face a major dilemma. As long as the killing is done somewhere else, out of sight, out of mind, why concern yourself?

Zimbabwe, fortunately, took a leaf out of Kenya's book, located rhino as quickly as possible and moved them out of danger areas onto private land as custodians, and today there are more black rhino in conservancies than on state land.

In spite of this, Zimbabwe today is losing their rhino in renewed poaching, as has been the case in Namibia over the past 10 years. Nowhere are rhino completely safe. Added to this is the number of park personnel directly involved in slaying rhino. Those game reserves that maintain high levels of security have seen poachers turn their attention to softer targets on occasion with the collusion of reserve staff. This is a betrayal of the highest magnitude.

Areas such as Tanzania, Zambia, Mozambique and many parts of Zimbabwe are vast and we know now what happened to their rhino populations. Just finding the rhino was difficult enough, let alone protecting them. The word 'stronghold', so often used in reference to Zimbabwe rhino programmes, had a most sad end, given all the effort that went into it. In hindsight, it was probably naïve to think we could protect that many rhino over such a vast area in the circumstances prevailing at the time.

Esmond Bradley Martin and Lucy Vigne writing in *SWARA*, the East African

Wildlife Society's journal of September/October 1992, stated: 'The Zimbabwe Department of National Parks and Wildlife management still believed they had 2 000 black rhino in the country in 1991 ... The shocking reality is that there are probably only 500 to 1 000 rhino left.'

The figure was actually under 500! The conservation world was stunned when the news became public.

There was no simple solution, given what Martin and Vigne further wrote:

There are three general reasons that rhino poaching has increased in Zimbabwe in the last year or so. First, the economy of Zambia had gone down further, giving a greater incentive for more poaching, while the Zambian authorities have been unable to prevent poachers from crossing the river border. Second, in Zimbabwe, the anti-poaching staff have become very wary; they now had poorer terms of service and there was not enough equipment nor people in the field. Third, in local currencies the value of rhino horn has gone up sharply, and the number of trade groups for the horn had increased. The horn was smuggled into Lusaka and then mostly taken by air to Swaziland or overland to South Africa for export to Taiwan.

To raise funds in support of Zimbabwe's efforts, in 1993 at Sabi Sabi Game Reserve, the REF launched a limited-edition print of an original painting of mine of a pair of black rhino. Julienne du Toit, a well-known and much-respected South African environmental writer, interviewed Glen Tatham at the launch and wrote the following in an article: 'The rhino has a face only a mother could love. And if it becomes extinct, can anybody say what a difference it will make in our everyday lives? But there's a bloody war being fought over these lumbering, half-blind creatures.'

In giving talks on rhino, I often pose the following question (admittedly usually the people in the audience don't own or work with rhino): 'Would you buy a very expensive sports car and leave it out in foul weather with the hood down.' The answer is a most emphatic 'no', but that is exactly what took place, especially in the private sector. Little or no security measures had been put in place, largely as a result of the decline in poaching since 1994 and the massive upsurge in private owners acquiring rhino. Most believed, thought or hoped the problem had gone away. We were all dead wrong; it had merely gone underground. The Chinese are very patient and knew they could draw on their own stock piles, but the dynamics have changed today with new role players and different reasons to acquire the horns.

FOLLOWING SPREAD: The 15 000 km² Okavango Delta in Botswana, home once again to both species of the African rhino. Photo: Wilderness Safaris/Dana Allen.

Changing mindset

I travelled to Zambia's Luangwa Valley in 1994, during which time we had the pleasure of having dinner with Phil Berry who at one stage had been the head of the task force in the battle to protect the rhino. The following day, over a few beers, I was to meet a gentleman who was employed by an aid organisation surrounding the park, and I asked him about the loss of the park's rhinos, knowing he worked with the communities. He lowered his voice and his head to the level of the bar and said, 'The promises made by government to the people living alongside this great system have never been forthcoming.' In his opinion, if all that stood between you and starvation was a well-stocked game reserve with an especially valuable animal such as a rhino, would you too not become a poacher? And of course the answer has to be 'yes'.

Pause for one moment and cast your mind back ... an area as vast as Luangwa must have been impossible to patrol – rhinos are spread out, limited staff, equipment, unbearable heat, tsetse flies, mosquitoes, and being up against armed and dangerous men. We know today that the cost of effectively covering large areas is very high. One only has to look at the Kruger National Park, where in 2011 alone they lost more than 200 rhino in spite of a military presence and being regarded as one of the best-equipped parks in Africa – and even they seem powerless to stem the tide at this point.

With the change of government and politics after 1994, the ESPU was finally disbanded in 2003. Furthermore, whether one wants to admit it or not, the state's desire for transformation resulted inevitably in a collapse of capacity and loss of experience with the move to create nine conservation agencies (one department for each of the provinces) that proved to be very costly.

By 1999 a great deal of the illegal killing of rhino had tailed off as a result of what had happened in Zimbabwe with the counter measures taken to stop the killing. The war did not spill over into South Africa as was believed would happen. But had the threat really gone away?

So much has been written about the fate of the rhino and what has befallen it in the past that one may be forgiven for asking the question: 'Was it all worthwhile?' There is a growing body of opinion in South Africa that the cost of protecting an animal such as the rhino is an expensive business. It is almost too costly. The mindset here is different. Game ranching has become a massive lucrative industry. If you are talking about the moral issue of saving an endangered species from extinction, I believe few would argue the point. However, how do you separate the moral issue from the economic one? Where is the money going to come from to protect such an animal? We are all fully aware that most African governments generally pay lip service when it comes to wildlife conservation. If it was not for the generosity of NGOs and the private sector, the situation as we know it today would be far worse. Does the end justify the means? Or is it possible the means justify the end?

The problem for the rhino is that we continue to deal with the *effect*, which we all agree requires immediate action and clearly is very costly. We have been there before and we can count our blessings that the rhino did survive. We are back again dealing with the *effect* and certainly the *cause* remains. The *cause* remains because the world has not yet adequately dealt with it, or simply does not want to, or will never be able to for multiple reasons. Somewhere in a number of far-off countries the desire for rhino horn continues as it has done so for centuries. We need, as a matter of urgency, to recognise this and take bold action even if it is anathema to most, usually in the west, that legalising the trade will spell the end for the rhino. Poaching of rhino for their horns will never be completely eradicated but that should not deter us from seeking ways to work with the *cause* rather than continue waging an endless war we will, it seems, never win.

When I first travelled to the US in 1973, there was a major worldwide campaign to save the tiger. More than 20 years later the tiger was back in the headlines (1994), and then back again in 2011, almost another 20 years later ... going through the same process all over again. The same conservation organisations are still at it, the same generous public are likewise footing the bill. A similar situation now exists Africa – in 1994 we were down to 2 400 black rhino and the prediction in some quarters was that the species would be extinct by 2025. At the end of 2016, the recorded number of both black and white rhino poached since 2008 stands at 7137.[2]

At the turn of the 19th century there were probably no more than 100 black rhino in South Africa, and today the latest figure from the African Rhino Specialist Group (AfRSG), March 2016, stands at 450 occurring in private reserves alone. That in itself is a massive achievement in spite of the onslaught since 2008. I would like to repeat that the private rhino owners are on their own with no state support whatsoever, and they bear all the costs of security – and that should change. The NGO movement should be encouraged to contribute and support private rhino owners. Help from the state is never going to be forthcoming. They continue to receive funding from well-meaning sources, but this is not going to be sustainable (for more information, see Chapter 4).

The dilemma the rhino now face is that they are considered by some as worth more dead than alive. If they are to survive, we are going to have to turn that belief around to ensure they are in fact far more valuable alive than dead.

CHAPTER 2

The threat –
know thy enemy

The threat – know thy enemy.

– GLEN TATHAM, CHIEF WARDEN OPERATIONS,
ZIMBABWE NATIONAL PARKS AND WILDLIFE, 1993

The rhino trade debate

Glen Tatham's words return to haunt us ... the ongoing killing of rhinoceros in South Africa, and in particular the Kruger National Park since 2008, is cause for considerable alarm. In attempting to combat the scourge, vast resources have been applied by the private sector, the state and through donations, amounting to over R400 million in Kruger alone. Yet 2013 saw an all-time high of 1 004 animals poached. This was subsequently eclipsed by the 2014 figure of 1 215, and in 2015 it was 1 175, of which no less than 826 came from within Kruger.

The rise in organisations focused on rhino conservation as a result of this onslaught has been impressive, but at the same time it has cast into question the legitimacy of some groups and the opportunistic nature of their fundraising. As more and more rhinos die, the emotion driving all this effort intensifies, but ultimately it will reach a saturation point where people start to question whether any of the effort is paying off, and willing donors will become exhausted.

Clearly the attempts to halt the rhino's decline have not entirely succeeded and are simply not sustainable in the long run, especially in large vulnerable parks and reserves flanked by high-density human populations. To be fair, the figure from 2016 does show a decline in rhino poached but this may well be attributed to the fact that the overall numbers have declined since 2008 and greater security has been ramped up.

A great deal of debate surrounds the question of the merits of a legal trade in rhino horn as a way to overcome the problem through a financial route. The controversy has involved a suite of talented economists, business people and conservationists proposing a legal trade. But there is a body of opinion diametrically opposed to the idea. These two opposing forces have been at loggerheads for decades, with neither position collectively tested in open debate outside the Convention on International Trade in Endangered Species (CITES). This is discussed in detail in Chapter 4.

The South African Department of Environmental Affairs (DEA) finally took the lead in March 2015 with the establishment of a committee of inquiry into the feasibility of a legal trade in rhino horn. Chaired by Nana Magamola, former chair of the Limpopo Environmental Authority, the appointed committee of 22 persons heard 54 presentations. To provide guidance on the matter, the committee of inquiry

OPPOSITE: A determined full on charge by a black rhino. Head down and eyes straining for movement is no doubt an experience that is most likely to arrest anyone's attention if the attacked person is on foot. Photo: Anthony Hall-Martin.

PREVIOUS SPREAD: The last two black rhino, a mother and calf, in mopane woodland in Savute, Botswana. Both were subsequently killed by poachers. Photo: Herman Potgieter.

then reported to an inter-departmental technical committee and an inter-ministerial committee appointed by cabinet, according to the minister. The recommendations, however, have not been made known to the public. The question is why not?

South Africa was scheduled to host the 17th convention of the parties to CITES, known as the CITES CoP17 summit, in Johannesburg in September 2016. In August 2016, the DEA announced that the South African government would not be submitting a proposal for trade in rhino horn to the summit. Our conclusion is that if South Africa played host to the CITES CoP17 summit, officials would be afraid of a possible backlash in their own backyard from the international community diametrically opposed to lifting the trade ban on rhino horn. The officials preferred to play for time as there is no doubt the matter will arise again.

Ahead of the conference, Susie Offord-Woolley, managing director of Save the Rhino International, wrote:

Tackling the trade in rhino horn requires a concerted effort from CITES members to cooperate and commit to tougher regulation and sentencing for criminals involved in the trade, as well as a commitment to tackling the trade at source – the consumer – through education and awareness programmes.[1]

The CITES CoP17 conference in Johannesburg, the largest ever with 3 500 delegates, was opened on 24 September 2016. Among other things, President Jacob Zuma said in his opening address that the government was tackling the issue of poaching: 'We have worked hard and our security strategy has resulted in a visible decline in the number of rhinos poached in 2016. Our law enforcement agencies work hard to break the illicit value chain of wildlife trafficking in South Africa and beyond.'

The evidence, however, suggests otherwise. The Friday before the conference began, spokesperson Musa Mntambo of Ezemvelo KZN Wildlife said poaching had continued that very week: 'On Tuesday we were standing at 107 [poached in 2016] and today we are at 115, which means we lost eight rhinos this week' – this in a 'flagship' park in the very heartland of rhino conservation in South Africa.[2]

Africa's rhino are dying but we learnt very little from CoP17 about solving the issue. So it's back to the drawing board and the same old scenario of dead poachers being sent back in pine boxes, increasing numbers of dead rhino, costly security ('intensive protection zones'), being constantly on a war alert, exhausted rangers, as well as heightened suspicion about the government's real ability to get on top of the many aspects that impact environmental crime where the principal victim is the rhino. We are not just talking about the enormous cost of security, which in itself is staggeringly expensive.

Any proposal put forward at any future CITES conferences concerning a legal trade is going to have to cross many hurdles to gain acceptance as the world at large is opposed to any form of trade. South Africa holds the bulk of Africa's rhino, yet on suggestions concerning lifting the ban, the world seeks to lay down the conditions; the world speaks the loudest, and has done so for decades. But the major international agencies are going to have to step up if they are genuinely concerned about survival of the species. We in southern Africa cannot fight this war alone.

Dr John Ledger, long-time colleague and former director of the Endangered Wildlife Trust (EWT), had the following to say:

> The mind-numbering utterances of the anti-trade animal rights' lobby and its mainstream media cheerleaders give little cause for hope that wildlife in Africa will flourish and endure in the future. A number of African states have been captured by Western governments and by the animal rights' activists. The public destruction of ivory and rhino horn in well-publicised media circuses tells Africans that elephants and rhinos have no value.
>
> Why don't we stop playing lethal, absurd games and get down to business by introducing a legal, controlled, transparent trade in rhino horn with China? It is surely the only sensible way to get out of the untenable situation we find ourselves in today.[3]

What actions emanated from CoP17 regarding the future of all five rhino species? The answer is nothing much.

So who's the enemy?

In 1960 I travelled to Tsavo National Park, which spans an area of 20 800 km² about 250 km from the port city of Mombasa. Africa then had an estimated 65 000 to 100 000 black rhino. Tsavo held some 9 000 of these animals during my 1960 visit. Upon my return with Dr Anthony Hall-Martin in 1980, by which time both of us were members of the IUCN's African Elephant Specialist Group, the total population of black rhino across Africa was less than 15 000. Our rhino colleagues were appalled, as was Dr Hall-Martin who represented both interests. I was there to discuss South Africa's dubious track record of facilitating movement of ivory from neighbouring countries to international markets.

In Tsavo National Park this area was named 'Rhino Valley' due to the high population of the species; poachers wiped them all out. Photo: Clive Walker.

The International Union for Conservation of Nature's (IUCN) African elephant and rhino specialist group meeting at Kilaguni Lodge, Tsavo National Park in 1980. The meeting revealed there were less than 15 000 black rhino remaining in Africa. Photo: Clive Walker.

By the 1980s, Tsavo had lost all of its 9 000 black rhino to Kalashnikov-wielding tribesmen. The rhino horn found its way to Mombasa and then onwards to Yemen, the Gulf States and China. The trail has since changed routes, and it now has a variety of sophisticated Southeast Asian destinations, managed by faceless individuals dealing in high-end contraband from the blood-soaked real estate of Africa. At one time Taiwan, with which the apartheid government nurtured a cosy relationship, was a leading Asian country involved in environmental crime, but no longer. Why not? The Taiwanese government took some serious action against the illegal trade. But others keep seeing opportunities for pillage, for example, by 2012 Vietnam had come to the fore, as reported in *The Guardian*:

> Conspicuous consumption from a growing middle class in Vietnam is driving the catastrophic poaching of rhino horns in South Africa, conservationists warned on Monday ... Lately it has become a party drink for corporate events and promoted on Vietnamese websites as 'the alcoholic drink of millionaires' when ground down and taken with wine.
>
> The Southeast Asian country comes bottom of a [World Wildlife Fund] scorecard of countries ranked on their prevention of illegal wildlife trade ... While trade in rhino horn has been illegal since 2006 and the law carries the threat of fines and up to seven years in prison, there is little enforcement in Vietnam ... Of 43 arrests of Asian nationals for rhino crimes in South Africa this year [2012], 24 were Vietnamese, according to a report by Tom Milliken, ivory trade expert at wildlife trade monitoring network TRAFFIC ... One of the main routes for rhino horn from Johannesburg to Hanoi is believed to be through Vietnamese on 'pseudo-trophy hunts' ... Between July 2009 and May 2012, 48% of such hunters in South Africa were Vietnamese nationals, Milliken's report notes.[4]

Several Vietnamese diplomats have been recalled after being caught with rhino horn in South Africa. In 2008, a Vietnamese diplomat, Vu Moc Anh, was filmed taking delivery of rhino horn outside the Vietnamese embassy in Pretoria.[5]

A modern form of neo-colonialism has invaded our shores. The quest to commandeer Africa's wealth has its source, not in Europe, but in Asia. Although anxious to be seen as helping Africa, in reality the players have other agendas.

What is the price of the number of foreign embassies that have opened and the number of Asians who have legitimately entered the country? Estimates suggest that between 300 000 and 500 000 Chinese nationals are present in the country, most of whom arrived after 1994.[6] Beyond the longstanding South African Indian community, Southeast Asians have been arriving from other countries – Pakistan,

Vietnam, South Korea, Cambodia and Thailand. In this process of opening up the country, we have also opened Pandora's Box. South Africa has become a haven and breeding ground for international crime syndicates, and criminals in turn find willing prey among the destitute, who have become participants in the slaughter of rhino.

In the 6th century BCE, the Chinese general and military strategist Sun Tzu observed: 'If you know your enemy and know yourself, you will not be imperilled in a hundred battles ... If you do not know your enemies nor yourself, you will be imperilled in every battle.'

As applies to so much of the world's endangered wildlife, Asia and especially China are the plunderers. They do little to stop the slaughter of their own wildlife by their citizens. Ancient Chinese literature clearly reveals the use of animal body parts in traditional Chinese medicine (TCM), but it does not stop there. Ivory is not used in medicine, and neither are the shark fins used to make soup that sells at staggering prices, decimating the populations of these top predators.

According to demographic figures, China has 1.3 billion people and growing. Theirs is an ancient civilisation with a proud and deep history bequeathed to the world. They have not been colonisers in the modern sense of the word, but rather have a centuries-long profile as inventors, traders, agriculturists, ocean-going travellers, artists, poets and writers. China is on the march, and it now has Africa in its sights. Yet we scarcely know our enemy.

The Chinese extractive culture of making money from natural resources knows no bounds. Their appetite for exotic health cures, art and animal objects, as well as foods, is part of this. It has been said that a nation is defined by what its people eat. Conservationists and the NGO movement would do well to study the Chinese more closely when it comes to their outlook on living or dead organisms as food or medicine. Their treatment of animals, both domestic and wild, is a revelation in the manner in which they are prepared for the dinner table.

In the main we have a Western outlook on these issues. We have a long history of attachment to other life forms. Skinning a snake alive or thrusting a live chicken into boiling water to remove its feathers is regarded as appalling cruelty. The

TOP LEFT: A Yemini displays his prized 'Jambia' ceremonial dagger. Handles were once made of rhino horn. Photo: Esmond Martin.

TOP RIGHT: The 'cause' of the crisis: a stock of raw rhino horn. Photo: Clive Walker.

BOTTOM LEFT: Field rangers of Liwonde National Park, Malawi, trained by South African National Parks who also restocked the park with black rhino. Photo: Clive Walker.

BOTTOM RIGHT: A Chinese medicine shop in Taiwan displays a raw rhino horn on the third shelf. Photo: REF Archive.

NGO movement is a Western concept, and these ideas are deeply ingrained in our thinking. But how do we even begin to understand or change the ways of an ancient civilisation? Do the Chinese simply not care how an animal is killed or where it comes from? It is doubtful that they or any other Southeast Asians will change their ways any time soon.

China has tremendous biodiversity: 562 mammal species, 1 269 birds, 403 reptiles and 346 amphibians. Many are endemic. But wildlife in China suffers from massive habitat destruction, pollution, and poaching for food, fur and body parts used as ingredients in TCM. More than 840 animal species are threatened, vulnerable or endangered as a consequence of these activities.[7] At a wildlife conference in Johannesburg in 2013, a prominent South African who had travelled to China noted that she was 'struck by the utter silence in the Chinese landscape'. 'Not even the sounds of birds,' she said.

China once had large numbers of elephants. Today there are around 300 in the Xishuangbanna and Pu'er prefectures of southern Yunnan. Poaching an elephant is a capital crime. The four remaining subspecies of tigers are critically endangered. The demand for tiger bones and fur, both used in TCM, is the principal threat facing all species of tigers, and that demand has now found a new mark in South Africa: lion bones. The snow leopard, clouded leopard and North China leopard are all protected by the state. The Père David's deer, of which only a few survived in captivity in China, was saved from extinction in the 19th century only because a number were held in European zoos and deer parks; a breeding programme in Europe eventually enabled the species to be returned to China in 1985.[8]

At least three species of extant Asian rhino once occurred in China, according to records and artwork from antiquity, but all were extinguished there early in the 20th century: Indian rhino (extinct in China since 1920); Sumatran rhino (1916); and Javan rhino (1922).[9] (For more on the Asian rhino, see Chapter 7.) With the disappearance of their own rhino a long time ago, the Chinese of course set about plundering their neighbours' rhino, encouraging local people to do the dirty work. The black rhino and more recently the white rhino of Africa are their greatest shame.

Once China and other Southeast Asian countries had nearly wiped out their own three species of rhino, they roped in their Middle Eastern neighbours, seafaring Arab traders who knew the East African coastline. Asian and Arab traders supplied guns to the war-torn Horn of Africa, replacing the bows and arrows of old. The 20th-century carnage of the African rhino and elephant was soon to begin.

How do lands with old cultures that have produced astonishing innovations, works of art, philosophy and architecture have no conscience about natural resources? Does the ordinary Chinese person care?

We seldom hear of any central figures in this illegal trade being brought to justice – usually only the local poachers, who may end up freed, out on bail, jailed, or in plain pine boxes. Many people are seriously concerned about our ANC government's cosying up to China with a growing trade relationship.

Conservationists in Africa cannot stem the onslaught alone. As a matter of urgency, we need the international community to apply pressure for changes through treaties and enforcement actions. Talk of altering mindsets is mostly just wishful thinking. The alternative, distasteful as it may seem, may eventually call for discussions of ways to feed the demand through a legal trade, rather than to continue opposing it and failing to stem the slaughter.

Corruption and the criminal justice system

In 2012 the number of poachers arrested in South Africa was 267. The figure for 2013 amounted to 343 and this increased by 12 per cent in 2014 to 386.[10] Similar figures have been rolled out for 2015 and 2016. More troubling, though, is that we seldom hear about action against the kingpins or middlemen, the African-based foreign nationals who serve as exporters and smugglers. The silence is deafening – there are very few arrests, let alone convictions. These people do not even appear in the statistics.

What has the government actually done to tackle and expose the sophisticated criminal syndicates operating within South Africa? Poachers are brought to trial … but there matters grind to a halt. It is therefore not surprising that suspicions exist of collusion among magistrates, officials, police officers and attorneys. The state needs to demonstrate either that this is not the case or that it is genuinely doing something about the matter. This is an area of grave concern in South Africa, especially given the 2016 upheaval within the National Prosecuting Authority.

As reported by Matthew Savides,[11] the Durban-based environmental activist Jamie Joseph submitted a report to the then Public Protector Thuli Madonsela, surrounding her concerns in KwaZulu-Natal. A spokesperson from her office, Kgalalelo Masibi, confirmed that the public protector was in the early stages of a preliminary investigation into how corruption was enabling rhino poaching.

Given the 7 245[12] rhino deaths since 2008, why has the government not tackled this issue? The elimination of the ESPU followed by the deliberate collapse of the Scorpions has had a great deal to do with the current state of affairs in South Africa. As Jamie Joseph states:

'We can have all the weapons in the world and all the anti-poaching dogs and all the helicopters, but if we lose the war on corruption, we lose the war on everything'.[13]

Joseph is in all probability dealing with the tip of the iceberg, but credit to her for voicing her opinion. Highly qualified, dedicated prosecutors and law enforcers within South Africa have their tasks made almost impossible by the widespread and rampant culture of corruption. Considering the many avenues of reviews and appeals to frustrate the law, it is difficult to gauge to what extent the justice system is compromised. The threat is not only from the East, but also from the corruption within South Africa. And we are not alone. As Kenly Greer Fenio stated: 'Political will and corruption play their part. While both countries now have official policies in place against poaching and trafficking, experts say implementation is fraught with complications because of corruption on multiple levels.'[14]

This is supported by a statement by savetherhino.org: 'Mozambique, as a key transit for smuggled rhino horn, causes South Africa the biggest headache due to its shared border with the Kruger National Park, home to the continents largest population of rhinos. A picture is painted of a country where corruption permeates all levels of society, and meaningful law enforcement is scarce.'[15]

An international report under the headline 'A Shameful Record: Official 2013 South African Rhino Poaching Stats' makes for very uncomfortable reading. The South African government simply has not shown the political will to address the situation as shown by President Zuma's opening address at the CoP17 summit.

The ever-increasing, state-level corruption has reached alarming proportions and is cause for grave concern in terms of inefficiency. Mangosuthu Buthelezi, leader of the Inkatha Freedom Party and former patron of the Rhino and Elephant Foundation (REF), has observed that corruption and maladministration are rife at all levels of government, reminding us of the saying that when a fish rots, the rot starts at the head.[16]

Many state institutions have serious question marks hanging over their performance. Speaking at the 2016 Mining Indaba in Johannesburg, AngloGold Ashanti Chairman Sipho Pityana said,

National Treasury has identified almost R26 billion in irregular expenditure at various levels of government in the last financial year [2014–15] alone. You might wonder how on earth a failure of governance on that scale is possible, but you need only look at the fact that about 72 per cent of government departments and SOEs [state-owned enterprises] are non-compliant with supply-chain management standards.'[17]

Soon afterwards *The Star* reported that the figure for the financial year 2015–16 had risen to an alarming R48 billion.

When the very organisation responsible for saving the rhino in the early 1960s – the Natal Parks Board, known today as Ezemvelo KZN Wildlife – has to rely on an international NGO for the provision of boots for field staff and for feed and veterinary care for their patrol horses, one has to wonder what in the world is going on.

Besides money disappearing, South Africa has seen the transformation of human resources since 1994, in the process losing valuable capacity. In the civil service this has led to a massive drain of highly skilled personnel. In the haste to transform the civil service, we have installed staff with a drastic lack of experience, and this comes at a high price. The irony here is that the state has wound up needing to spend billions since 1994 on consultants – largely drawn from among those who were previously employed by the state.

Did we learn any lessons from the last rhino wars that barely touched us (discussed in Chapter 1)? It seems not. We are repeating history – throwing lots of money at trying to save the rhino, but still dealing with the effects of the crisis and not its cause: the endless Asian desire to acquire rhino horn for various purposes. Sensible people would sit down to debate the merits of supplying or not supplying that desire. It is a much-needed debate.

The rhino is a kind of barometer – measuring the pressure – can we turn the situation around? Lose the rhino, and we lose something of ourselves.

The challenge is not how we manage rhino but how we manage human actions. And yet for the moment, we have no choice but to deal with the effects of the crisis.

Other effects on the rhino crisis

It is important to remember how the socio-political and economic conditions that currently prevail in South Africa have affected the present rhino crisis. These conditions have bearing when dealing with an animal that has the misfortune of carrying on the end of its nose a horn prized almost beyond comprehension. Close to 50 years of apartheid government, from 1948 to 1994, were abhorrent, cruel, and a blot on our country's history. But South Africa today is not the South Africa of the past. After 23 years of democracy our human landscape has dramatically changed. Yes, we have a constitution that ranks among the world's most progressive. Given a greatly expanded civil service with high salaries, social grants to some 16 million people, better housing and electricity, freedom of speech, and a suite of civil liberties, life for many people has certainly improved. But for the majority we remain a terribly unequal society.

In 1980 South Africa's human population was 21 million – today it is 56 million. Politicians prefer not to discuss this or how it impacts on the natural world. According to the World Economic Forum, South Africa has the third-highest rate of unemployment in the world – more than 50 per cent. Nearly 12 million of the country's 18.6 million children live in poverty. Four out of 10 children live in households where none of the adults work. According to census records, it is estimated that between 5 and 8 million illegal immigrants have entered South Africa since 1994.[18]

One reason the crisis is so difficult to contain is that, although South Africa is a wealthy country, the inequality between the rich and the poor is among the highest in the world. We have desperately poor communities living alongside well-stocked game reserves. At ground zero, poverty and unemployment levels are extremely high: 8.3 million unemployed with clearly no short- to medium-term solutions. South Africa's poor are drawn into the rhino saga as collateral damage. What is the price of the returns to CEOs and shareholders that override benefits to workers, communities, the environment and the national interest?

PREVIOUS SPREAD: Zebra grazing on a grass-covered flood plain in the Okavango Delta. One of the top Wilderness Safari tented camp operations can be seen in the background. Photo: Wilderness Safaris/Dana Allen.

Failure in community engagement

Community involvement and education are key elements in this battle, although how much they can achieve in the short term is questionable. This does not mean these efforts should be abandoned, but rather that we should study successful operations and emulate them. We are conserving rhino for everyone, and when we regard the communities around the parks as valuable allies, we can invest accordingly.

However, slippage happens. Poaching of the desert-adapted rhino in Namibia's Kunene province – 392 animals lost in the past 10 years, half of those in the last 2½ years, and a good number in the community area to the west of Etosha National Park – revealed a shocking reversal of the prior success of state- and community-based involvement in conservation in that region of Namibia.[19] We asked one of the principal NGOs supporting conservation of the desert-adapted rhino for views on the situation and received this response: 'I can't really comment on anything that has been reported in the media – sorry, need to maintain good relations with our contacts at MET [Ministry of Environment and Tourism]!'

The difficulty for any NGO, and even for members of the press, is that the rhino situation has become so sensitive that poking your nose into the hornet's nest can mean doors being slammed in your face, or worse. Read the disclaimer attached to emails from anyone at SANParks; it clearly illustrates the need for all concerned to be very careful what they say.

Minister Edna Molewa of South Africa's DEA has said, 'We are particularly proud of our conservation record, being home to more than 80 per cent of the world's remaining black and white rhino'.[20] Her claim about the conservation track record sadly ignores the number of rhino slain in state protected areas. She also neglected to mention the number of poachers arrested for poaching inside the Kruger National Park, which was 315 in 2015 alone, excluding 103 from the western boundary. This is the very area that has received major support for at least 15 years, where community programmes were already under way when I joined the SANParks Board in 1999.

The DEA press release on 1 November 2015, which referred to President Jacob Zuma addressing more than 5 000 community members from Nkomazi and Bushbuckridge at the Skukuza soccer stadium, emphasised the important role that communities can play in the fight against rhino poaching. 'I would like to take this opportunity to appeal to all communities living close to conservation areas, to be aware of the threats of rhino poaching. Many of you are aware of the ability of unscrupulous poaching syndicates to exploit vulnerable people in your communities by offering large amounts of money to kill and dehorn rhino or elephant. We can all do something to stop that – by blowing the whistle on all wildlife criminals. As

TOP LEFT: Young men from the community area of Bakenberg in the Waterberg. Tourism, recreation-related activities, game farming and hunting hold some of the best prospects for them in a country with increasing unemployment. Photo: Clive Walker.

BOTTOM LEFT: A life of collecting firewood holds little hope for this young boy. If there is any long-term prospect for the future of wildlife, ways to make the lives of those living alongside 'wild' areas meaningful must be found. Photo: Clive Walker.

TOP RIGHT: A tin house and a vegetable garden may be this woman's only possessions. The Lapalala Wilderness School's Eco-Schools programme of vegetable gardening does make a meaningful difference. Most often it may be no more than a simple need that one can fill. Photo: Clive Walker.

BOTTOM RIGHT: A mother sits alongside her two children at her makeshift roadside vegetable stall. How do you reconcile her position with that of a well-stocked game farm down the road? Can anyone be surprised when the question is asked: are rhinos more important than people? Photo: Clive Walker.

proclaimed on World Rhino Day. We can all stand up and proclaim, no more,' [21]

Speaking to *News24* reporter Paul Herman in 2016 after addressing parliament, SANParks large-mammal ecologist Dr Sam Ferreira said, 'Those driving organised crime were targeting people around the parks. Many of them were displaced due to the implementation of the Group Areas Act during apartheid, and had suffered financially as a result.' He further noted that the security efforts, while showing results, were not sustainable in the long run. 'The key,' he insisted, 'was to disrupt organised crime.' [22]

General Johan Jooste (whose role is addressed in Chapter 4) put it to me this way: 'One needs to peel the onion from the outside.' As Dr Ferreira stated, problems derive in part from the Group Areas Act, but it is also true that by now SANParks has had 23 years since the advent of democracy to address the matter. Minister Edna Molewa is a hardworking, dedicated individual and no doubt sincere in her desire to see poaching curtailed, but the matter goes far beyond her own department and her equally concerned staff. Given South Africa's dismal track record of pseudo-rhino hunts, state employees involved in rhino poaching, canned lion hunting, and illegal harvesting of cycads, birds, reptiles and marine resources, we should not be too surprised when community engagement efforts stumble.

Dr Michael Knight, chair of the African Rhino Specialist Group (AfRSG), commented to private rhino owners in 2016 about:

> ... the unscrupulous South African wildlife ranchers, veterinarians, outfitters and professional hunters, who have colluded with Asian nationals to make rhino horn illegally available. This continues to damage the reputation of South Africa as a responsible and innovative wildlife country. A few are undermining the success of the wildlife industry as a whole and dare I say even bringing sustainable use – a cornerstone of the South African constitution – into question by those not supportive of it for ideological or ill-informed reasons. [23]

For conservation to include future participation by and benefits for communities, we need to be very mindful of Dr Knight's words, for at present the very term 'sustainable use' is anathema to many. Indeed, reports about good cooperation with Mozambican counterparts risk making us a laughing stock. They seem a transparent attempt to stave off comments, such as Julius Malema's claim that black people are worth less than rhinos.

Good intentions notwithstanding, it is perhaps naïve to believe that community engagement holds the key to being seen as working in the best interests of all South Africans; the massive publicity surrounding rhino conservation makes it come across as a 'white thing'. This aspect has haunted the government since the beginning of democracy. To be fair, serious, dedicated efforts to reverse this perception have been undertaken. But they have overlooked one crucial issue: the present value of rhino horn.

In a country that suffers from poor leadership, massive unemployment, a faltering economy, and a huge disparity between rich and poor that feeds resentment, who is going to maintain the costly upkeep of rhino, the kind of protection that inevitably invites comments about rhinos being more important than people?

No one wants to discuss corruption and nepotism, but put yourself in the position of someone with a large family to support and no possibility of employment, living in a tin house, alongside a well-stocked national park. For community engagement programmes to succeed, we have to be investing in changing people's lives, not merely their perceptions. In Kenya, Zimbabwe, Namibia and Botswana there are places where this is succeeding, where state and private rhino owners are doing magnificent work. The international and local rhino NGOs need to know this is possible and that it is being done in South Africa too.

We as authors mention the value of investing in 'changing people's lives'. But what exactly do we mean by this? The state conservation authorities and the private sector need to move this item right up to near the top of the agenda for the simple reason that unless we have the long-term support of 'communities', we are not going to win the battle or the war.

Let us look at an example: the village of Lesideng is the formal and informal settlement adjacent to the small village of Vaalwater in the Waterberg. There are two primary schools with a total of 3 200 children. One of the schools has a library but there are no library books; the other has no library and no books. Few, if any, of these children have ever been to a game reserve, let alone seen a rhino. With the assistance of Biblionef South Africa, these two schools and 35 other rural schools in the region now have the start of a library. That is what we mean by investing in people's lives, investing in literacy so that in the long term children will see the world differently.

TOP: The key to most misunderstandings concerning the environment is the role environmental education can play at the primary and secondary school levels in South Africa. South Africa is blessed with many fine NGO institutions who fortunately fill that void, but they need support and to push for a government that moves the item top and centre of the agenda. Photo: Clive Walker.

BOTTOM: The best way to a child's mind and heart is through books and reading. Lapalala Wilderness School (LWS), Save the Waterberg Rhino (STWR) and the CW Foundation working through the publisher of this book, Carol Broomhall, the Cape Town-based Biblionef donated enough books in the local SaPedi dialect for 38 schools in the rural Waterberg areas to start their libraries. LEFT TO RIGHT: Lucas Ngobeni from LWS, educator Natassja Benjamin, Nokuthula Mbenyane from Biblionef, principal Buzi Ester Moshupya, Jessica Babich from STWR, Clive Walker and Mashudu Makhokha, director of the LWS. Photo: Patrick Bonior.

Security implications regarding the protection of a valuable animal

Maintaining rhino in reserves – state or private – is obviously destined to fail without adequate protection. Security coupled with high-level monitoring is essential. This is critical in the case of the black rhino, where observations on populations are of paramount importance. In the 2014–15 financial year, the Department of Environmental Affairs (DEA), the Green Scorpions, Ezemvelo KZN Wildlife and the Peace Parks Foundation received a staggering amount of funding from outside donors in an effort to halt the slaughter of rhino – it was almost half a billion rand, of which a good percentage went into Kruger, as reported by Pearlie Joubert.[24] We feel that guarding a species in the 2-million-hectare Kruger National Park is simply not sustainable in the long term, given the park's extended border with Mozambique to the east and the high-density settlements to the west.

Often overlooked in favour of laying blame on neighbouring communities and Mozambique is that some of the killing in Kruger emanates from within the park itself, in collusion with outsiders. When a ranger, guide and gardener from a top Kruger camp were arrested for killing a white rhino in October 2014, a university student asked me, 'Is it a matter of falling standards?' It is about temptation, of course. The money realised from a pair of horns is considerable, and begs the question about two decades of effort at 'involvement of communities'. These men are from the local communities, they are not from Mozambique. In short, the massive upsurge of poaching in Kruger since 2008 gives a grim and ironic new meaning to the idea of 'involving communities'.

Another recent incident involved a regional ranger and a veterinary assistant in the north-west of Kruger who were caught red-handed while poaching a rhino using a hunting rifle and an axe. All these perpetrators may well have visited the park 20 years before as young children, and their parents may be beneficiaries of poverty relief efforts, but they remain subject to temptation. One can perhaps understand somebody with a very low income-generating job considering poaching, but what about a regional ranger with a good job and a position of significant responsibility and trust? Getting this position calls for integrity and some 15 years of service with the organisation. What possesses an individual to undertake such an act of betrayal and risk such a potentially distinguished career? And what does this do for staff morale?

'Betrayal' is a strong word, but it certainly applies. Game rangers are at the forefront in the battle to save rhinos and elephants. They are up against well-armed, dangerous individuals who are adept at killing rhino and equally adept at putting up a fight against any opposition. The outlaws have family and friends who must be aware of what they are doing, and who out of loyalty are complicit and sworn to secrecy. Rangers too have family in these communities, and people talk, and talk can be life threatening. Intimidation is far reaching, like the tentacles of an octopus.

Moreover, the job of a ranger does not end at 5 pm. It never ends, and neither does the stress that accompanies the work. They know they may be killed or may have to kill. Like soldiers, rangers have to deal with daily patrols and frequent contacts, and they cannot just close their computers and go home after a day's work. They are constantly confronting thoughts about the possibility of dying or of having to kill someone; as noted in the poaching timeline, 500 people were killed by anti-poaching units from 2010 to 2016.[25] Finding that one of your own has betrayed the core values of a ranger reflects on every ranger.

At an early stage of this rhino war figures were released about 'poacher' deaths while trying to kill rhino but this is no longer the case and we have not been able to trace any 'official' source that gives an accurate figure. No one, we believe, wants to discuss the matter, which is understandable as it is a very sensitive issue. It is not only rhino that are dying in this battle but people. Innocent people may well be victims as well, as reported by a 21-year-old unemployed male from Justica near the Kruger Park; 'If you have a death wish you can (report poachers) but I won't do that. I value my life'.[26]

We believe that parks and reserves without adequate leadership and sufficient capacity and resources to protect their rhino should remove or sell every animal. This advice should be applicable to the private sector as well, although it cannot be enforced there, and the choice falls to owners. Learning from successful operations, the best option is to place rhino in intensive protection zones (IPZs) away from reserve borders and away from human settlements. This point about IPZs was raised in question time at the Private Rhino Owners Association (PROA) meeting in August 2012, and owners were urged to give it serious consideration. Clearly Kruger security was not working, and park officials were urged to consider IPZs or remove animals. This security cordon finally started to get under way in 2015, by which time the overall death toll of rhino for South Africa was close to 5 000.[27]

For this kind of intensive approach to security to work, consideration should also be given to requiring that all future sales of rhino, both white and especially black, will be conditional upon the new owner demonstrating that prescribed security arrangements are in place. Failure to meet these requirements will put both the owner and the rhino at great risk. Rhino conservation has become a very expensive undertaking, and efforts must be strengthened to make rhino owners aware of these costs. Park Manager Tony Conway of iSimangaliso Wetland Park in KwaZulu-Natal, a former colleague in the AfRSG, provided us with up-to-date cost estimates in July

2015. To protect rhino in a state-owned protected area in South Africa requires one ranger per 10 km² = $4 426 (±R60 000) per km² per year in a 40 000-hectare (or 400-km²) park. A park of this size would thus require 40 field rangers. For more information see Chapter 4.

Such an operation is not even remotely possible in today's economic climate. This is the strongest argument the PROA makes in regard to their stated aim of pushing for a legal trade in rhino horn. The argument is that neither the state nor the private sector can afford this scenario into the future, and the rest of the world – all those people who do not carry the responsibility for conserving rhino, but who are by far the loudest opponents of a legal trade – will wind up bearing much of the blame for the demise of the species. According to PROA chair Pelham Jones, in an overview of South African privately owned reserves with rhino populations, the dilemma they have had to face looks like this:

As contained in the DEA-funded PROS/RMG survey carried out among private rhino reserves in mid-2015, some 5 837 or 33% of the white rhino national population and 450 or 28% of the black rhino national population (total 6 287 animals) are found in 330 known private reserves, comprising 2 million hectares.

- 50% intend to maintain populations but will not buy any further animals.
- 17% intend to sell 75% of their rhino populations if not already sold.
- 9% intend to sell between 25% and 75% of their rhino populations.
- 12% intend to purchase more rhino.

The survey further found that about 70 of the original 330 rhino reserves no longer have rhino; 80% had suffered poaching incidents; there had been 280 instances of threats to human life; and 369 kg of horn stolen in 27 different incidents. More than 1 000 rhino had been poached on private reserves.[28]

The vital role played by the private rhino owner

As the survey numbers from Pelham Jones indicate, some serious introspection is required, and indeed has been going on. Rhino owners have one option they can do something about, but it comes at a huge cost, and that is to ensure that they provide adequate budgets to handle the security of their rhinos.

A component of this is the question of intelligence gathering and a high-level scrutiny of all staff. Remember the enemy may well lie within, as the large parks have found. This is no longer 1993, when a rhino horn was worth US$100–150 per kg to the poacher. In turn, the person who organised the gang in Lusaka in the 1990s would sell the horns to traders for US$300–500 per kg. The overseas wholesaler would pay from US$750–1 000 per kg, and middlemen and medicine shops in the East paid about US$1 800 per kg.[29]

In 2012/13 rhino horn brought in the order of US$65 000 per kg (±R865 000) or more from the wholesaler. It is necessary to be careful in quoting figures, however. This dropped to US$35 000 in 2015 and the poacher would have been paid around US$2 150 per kg. The figure of US$65 000 per kg continues to be widely used in the media today but should be treated with caution. However, compared to prices paid to a poacher back in 1993 the increase is nevertheless staggering.[30]

The AfRSG and the WWF Rhino Range Expansion Programme have suggested continuing to encourage the spread of rhino onto community land as 'critical to expanding range and keeping numbers growing rapidly'. This objective may well be considered unwise today as the required budgets for security assessments and long-term sustainability are not in place to protect the translocated animals. Ignoring this is merely tantamount to condemning more and more rhino to the same fate as all those poached to date.

The WWF Range Expansion Programme is important in looking at suitable reserves of at least 20 000 hectares capable of taking a large group of black rhino in one introduction spread over a number of days. This has been successfully implemented in places in South Africa, with stock originating from the Eastern Cape and KwaZulu-Natal, but by no means all attempts have succeeded.

Tourism is held up as the way forward, but here the danger comes from the high expectations attached to owning such an animal. There is no point putting these animals onto community land without the necessary infrastructure, staff, good tourism potential, professionally trained personnel and, need I say, the finances to support upkeep and security costs. A combination of state, private sector and community participants would be the most desirable. This, however, is not easy to achieve with tourism as the only source of income. If there is no opportunity for trophy hunting, and the horn cannot be sold, we have eliminated the generation of any income other than via tourism.

Unless tourism is already established, the cost of making it so is prohibitively high. Most lodges in the three- to four-star category struggle to make profits.[31] Tourism is cyclical and is affected by disease, terrorism, floods and currency fluctuation, to name but a few factors. High-end lodges do make profits, but they are the minority because they invest heavily in infrastructure, training, marketing, and above all the right product delivered by the best people experienced in the business. A lodge in the middle of nowhere with half a dozen rhino is bound to fail.

There are no easy answers, but our belief is that the private landowner will play a major role in the future of rhino conservation, in a combination of ways. The key lies in their working both with the state and local communities. There is good work going on across many broad fronts and one aspect of this book is to portray this work. The situation can be greatly improved by dedicated activities that benefit people in surrounding communities, so that conserving wildlife is genuinely beneficial across the continent and not just a pastime of the rich.

We are fortunate to have Yolan Friedmann, CEO of the EWT, providing one opinion in the Afterword to this book, and we need to heed her words carefully. Rhino are not the only species at risk. They grab the headlines and have become an emotive subject, but they are only one component in this complex web. This rhino war is seriously eroding funding that should otherwise be supporting biodiversity conservation. We need to look at the entire picture, and that includes the people – because people need nature.

South Africa knows all about extinction as most of the country's wildlife disappeared during the 17th and 18th centuries. We have been there before and turned the situation around. I have no doubt we can do it again for the rhino. No other country in Africa has a conservation fraternity with the same depth of commitment and passion for the animal that South Africa has shown. The time has come when discussions on trade are detracting from our efforts on the ground to slow the poaching. In all probability, we will need a combination of all three areas of concern:

- The costs of protection
- The role of communities (including conservation NGOs, private owners and reserve neighbours)
- A serious attempt by government to address the legal aspects and corruption in the criminal justice system

Individually and separately we will not achieve the objective.

We have seen meeting after meeting after meeting. It is immensely frustrating that over the alarming years since 2008, the various NGOs, international associations, government parks and agencies, and in particular the IUCN AfRSG, have not come up with any effective solutions. The pro-trade lobby at least believe they have part of the answer.

It's a bleak picture in so many ways. The solution? There has to be one. The battle has been raging for far too long. We need to win this war once and for all.

TOP: Field rangers from various reserves in the Waterberg undergoing fitness training. They are the frontline defenders in the battle against wildlife crime on which so much depends. Photo: Clive Walker.

BOTTOM: Control points on access roads around conservancy areas have proved to play a major role in combating crime at many levels, including potential rhino poachers. Manned 24/7, these units check any vehicle entry. Cooperation through local community police forums is essential. Photo: Herc Hoffman.

In conclusion

Susie Offord-Woolley, managing director of Save the Rhino International, UK, has this to say on the subject:

In February 2016, Save the Rhino, US Fish and Wildlife Service, International Rhino Foundation and the UK's Department for Environment, Food and Rural Affairs joined together to fund the African Rhino Specialist Group's conference in the Kruger National Park in South Africa, which takes place every 2–3 years. This involves bringing approximately 80 experts, including country rhino coordinators, together. This is a very rare opportunity for people working in the field, conducting policy or research, working in demand reduction, and conservation donors to come together to share information, the latest research and techniques and set priorities.[32]

The specialist group used to be very focused on the biological management of rhinos, population numbers, their distribution and projections for growth. But the 2016 conference demonstrated how far we have come in such a short time. It had people and organisations from the widest selection of industries. People working in technology, intelligence, finance, social sciences and more are now involved in tackling rhino poaching.[33]

The EWT staged the first of a number of highly visible conferences at the University of Pretoria with over 200 delegates over 40 years ago. There were 24 papers presented over two days. Only one was about rhino and this was presented by Peter Hitchins, who at the time was a lone voice in the rhino wilderness. Hitchins's paper revealed that there were 402 black rhino in Zululand, 30 in the Kruger National Park and 10 in the Addo Elephant Park. It pays to look back and remind ourselves just how far we have come and where we are today.

All this is most commendable, but we all need to ask one very important question going forward. How do we halt or rapidly slow the killing down to manageable levels before the rhinos start a slow but dangerous descent into extinction?

Within the pages of this book there are positive steps that are being taken across many fronts to prevent this happening. We should not be deterred in this battle, which has been waging for nearly 10 years now, and we urge and encourage the AfRSG and those supporting it to become far more vocal and visible. Review the tables in this book that are presented by the AfRSG and TRAFFIC and take solace in the fact that we are far, far better off than we were in 1975 and way better than we were at the turn of the 19th century.

Source: Emslie, R.H., Milliken, T., Talukdar, B., Ellis, S., Adcock, K., Knight, M.H. 2016. African and Asian rhinoceroses – status, conservation and trade. A report from the IUCN Species Survical Commission (IUCN/SSC) African and Asian Rhino Specialist Groups and TRAFFIC to the CITES Secretariat pursuant to Resolution Conf. 9.14 (Rev. CoP15). Report to CITES 16th meeting (Johannesburg, September–October 2016), CoP 17 Doc.68 annex 5: 1–21.

REPORTED AFRICAN RHINO POACHING MORTALITIES 2006–2015

Country	2006	2007	2008	2009	2010	2011	2012	2013	2014	2015	2006–15 Total	2008–12	2013–15
Botswana	-	-	-	-	-	-	2	2	-	-	4	0.1%	0.1%
DR Congo	-	-	2	2	-	-	-	-	-	-	4	0.2%	0.0%
Kenya	3	1	6	21	22	27	29	59	11	11	214	4.8%	2.8%
Malawi	-	-	-	-	-	-	2	1	1	1	6	0.1%	0.1%
Mozambique	-	9	5	15	16	10	16	15	13	13	118	2.9%	1.2%
Namibia	-	-	-	2	2	1	`	4	90	90	130	0.3%	3.3%
South Africa	36	13	83	122	333	448	668	1004	1175	1175	5097	76.2%	89.6%
Swaziland	-	-	-	-	-	2	-	-	-	-	3	0.1%	0.0%
Tanzania	-	-	2	-	1	2	2	-	2	2	11	0.3%	0.1%
Uganda	-	-	-	-	-	-	-	-	-	-	-	0.0%	0.0%
Zambia	-	1	-	-	-	-	-	-	-	-	1	0.0%	0.0%
Zimbabwe	21	38	164	39	52	42	31	38	50	50	495	15.1%	2.9%
Total	60	62	262	201	426	532	751	1123	1342	1342	6083	2172	3789
Poached/day	0.16	0.17	0.72	0.55	1.17	1.46	2.05	3.08	3.63	3.68			

Timeline of significant rhino events

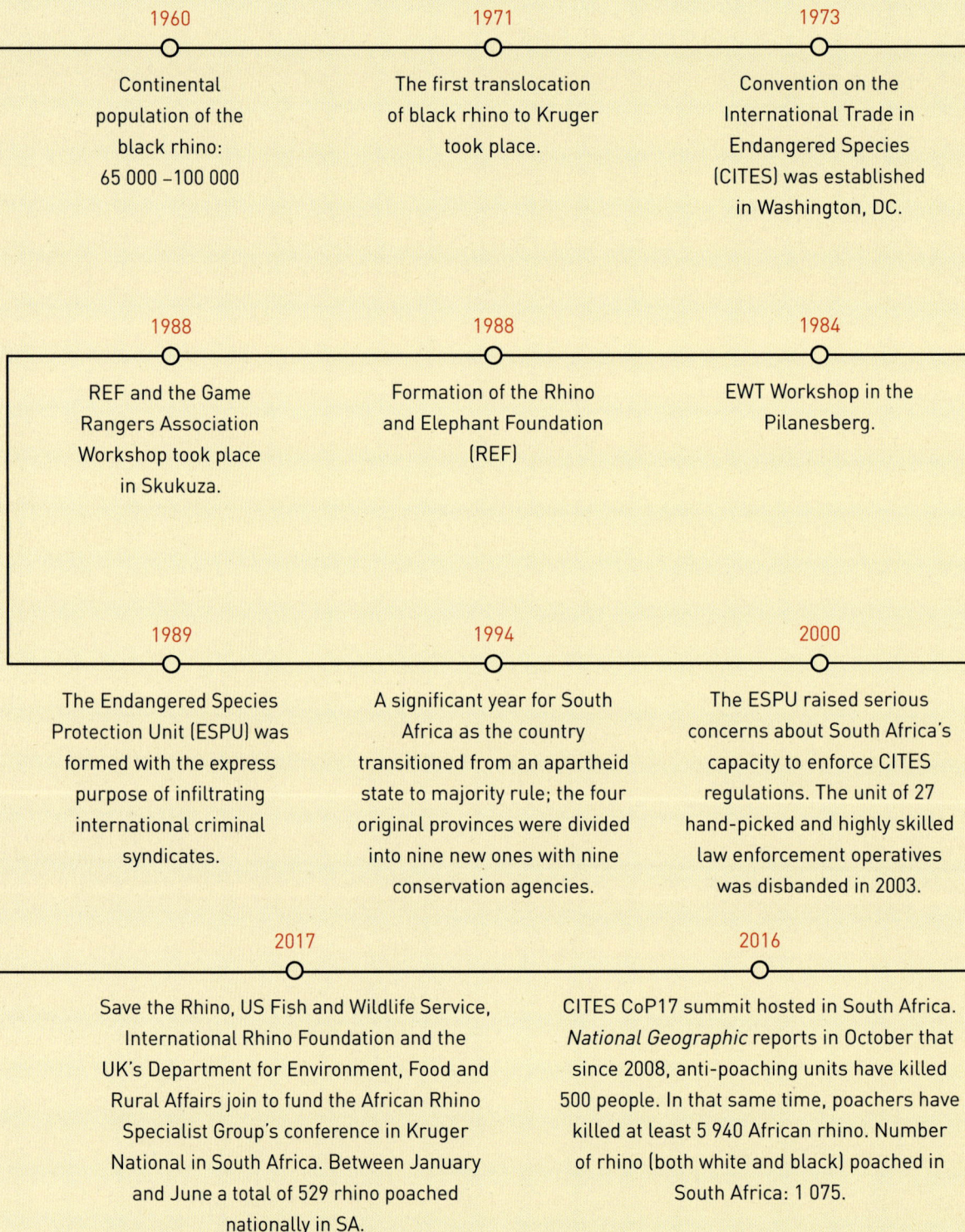

1960
Continental population of the black rhino: 65 000 –100 000

1971
The first translocation of black rhino to Kruger took place.

1973
Convention on the International Trade in Endangered Species (CITES) was established in Washington, DC.

1988
REF and the Game Rangers Association Workshop took place in Skukuza.

1988
Formation of the Rhino and Elephant Foundation (REF)

1984
EWT Workshop in the Pilanesberg.

1989
The Endangered Species Protection Unit (ESPU) was formed with the express purpose of infiltrating international criminal syndicates.

1994
A significant year for South Africa as the country transitioned from an apartheid state to majority rule; the four original provinces were divided into nine new ones with nine conservation agencies.

2000
The ESPU raised serious concerns about South Africa's capacity to enforce CITES regulations. The unit of 27 hand-picked and highly skilled law enforcement operatives was disbanded in 2003.

2017
Save the Rhino, US Fish and Wildlife Service, International Rhino Foundation and the UK's Department for Environment, Food and Rural Affairs join to fund the African Rhino Specialist Group's conference in Kruger National in South Africa. Between January and June a total of 529 rhino poached nationally in SA.

2016
CITES CoP17 summit hosted in South Africa. *National Geographic* reports in October that since 2008, anti-poaching units have killed 500 people. In that same time, poachers have killed at least 5 940 African rhino. Number of rhino (both white and black) poached in South Africa: 1 075.

1975

The CITES Convention came into force.

1975–1999

South Africa held an enviable record for the protection of rhino.

1976

Endangered Wildlife Trust conference on endangered wildlife in South Africa.

1981

China banned imports of rhino horn.

1980

IUCN rhino and elephant meeting in Tsavo National Park, Chaired by Sir Peter Scott. Kenya. Meeting advised the continental population of black rhino was down to 15 000. It was around this time that the AfRSG came into being chaired by Dr Kes Hillman.

1977

CITES granted both species of African rhino (white and black) the highest level of protection.

2003

WWF black rhino range expansion programme starts.

2005

20 rhino poached in the Kruger National Park.

2008

South Africa faces its own rhino war.

2015

Minister Edna Molewa appoints a Committee of Inquiry into the feasibility of a legal trade in rhino horn. DEA-funded PROS/RMG survey carried out among private rhino reserves.

2013

General Johan Jooste, a retired SADF military officer is appointed by Minister Edna Molewa as Officer Commanding Special Projects. Initial focus was to convert the Ranger Corps into an anti-poaching unit.

2010

Poaching appears to be out of control, driven by criminal syndicates in South Africa and Southeast Asia.

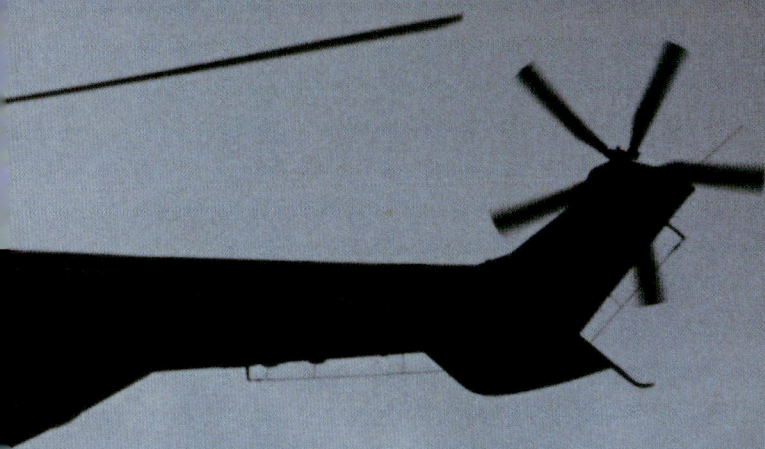

CHAPTER 3

Moving to save the rhino

The process by which an unsuspecting rhinoceros can be interrupted in its daily habits, attacked in the centre of the territory which it has painstakingly marked out a trail of urine and faeces, rendered unconscious, bound and then airlifted to a distant wilderness, there to be released and encouraged to resume the daily grind, is swift, extremely expensive and as unmarred by self-criticism as the building of the Ark.

– PATRICK MARNHAM, *FANTASTIC INVASIONS*

Intervention and lateral thinking

Rhino will not be saved in isolation to people, regardless of the fact that we are their biggest threat and, interestingly, their only saviour. Intervention and lateral thinking has to take place, and rather than harping on about the ongoing scenario of bloodied, hornless-faced rhino lying in pools of blood, we have to remain positive. We are caught in a dilemma here of massive proportions, and rhino numbers are declining at a rate above recruitment and no doubt will continue to do so. But at some point the pendulum must swing back to centre – how we get there is the big question.

Some serious introspection needs to be done about where rhino are currently located (by and large in state reserves). The best examples are the Kruger National Park and the Hluhluwe/Imfolozi Park in KwaZulu-Natal. Both are rated among the best in Africa in terms of habitat; however, they are both located in critical zones. Kruger has a 360-kilometre border with Mozambique from where the bulk of poaching has emanated, as well as a burgeoning human tide on its western boundary where fortunately they have a good number of private reserves within the Greater Kruger acting as a buffer zone. The two KwaZulu-Natal reserves are islands in a sea of humanity boxed in on all sides.

To re-enforce this view, these two reserves sustained a massacre of disturbing proportions during May 2017 of nine rhino poached in 48 hours, during a full moon. According to Tony Carnie, reporting in the *Sunday Times*: 'The latest killings in the Hluhluwe/Imfolozi Park have pushed the death toll in the province to at least 89 in the first 18 weeks of this year.'[1]

It is our considered opinion that it is not sustainable in the long run for each of these areas to maintain the defence that is required to protect large populations of rhino. Even if the authorities do not like or want to admit it, they are not only losing the battle, but also the war.

Across South Africa and the world there has been the most incredible ground-swell support from donors to help ... and yet the killing continues.

OPPOSITE: A white rhino gazes intently at one of the highly trained dogs and its handler in an unnamed reserve. Dogs have proved to be essential in detecting smuggled rhino horn, tracking poachers and as attack dogs. The cost to train these dogs is considerable and the Endangered Wildlife Trust are at the forefront of this activity. Photo: Chris Serfontein.

PREVIOUS SPREAD: A Puma SAAF helicopter lifts a black rhino in a net from the scene of capture to the rhino bomas somewhere in Zululand, KwaZulu-Natal. South Africa can pride itself in having a reputation unequalled in the world regarding the movement of large wildlife species. Photo: The South African Veterinary Association.

Is the rhino worth saving?

Professors Melville and Andrea Saayman of the North-West University posed the following question (2016): 'Is the rhino worth saving?'[2]

Let us start by looking at the South African R10 note. It depicts a white rhinoceros – important enough to place on the country's currency and a 'must-see' member of the Big 5 when visiting South Africa.

In 1990 the country had one million visitors, and today that figure is in the region of 10 million. This figure nevertheless needs to recognise that not all these visitors are 'tourists', but rather that more than 3 million so-called 'tourists' from neighbouring countries are, according to 2015 data, in fact 'on shopping trips'.[3] The top attraction for the genuine tourist is the country's wildlife, especially the Big 5.

The North-West University undertook several surveys to determine the various components that constitute the value of rhino, according to the Saaymans. The surveys were carried out in the Kruger National Park, which has the highest concentration of white rhino in Africa. Tourists were asked how much they were willing to pay to view a rhino. The amount over a three-year period (2010–2013) added up to between US$5.9 million and US$14.9 million. Based on the estimated number of rhino at the time, which was given as 13 000 white rhino, it implies a value between US$150 000 and US$450 000 per animal per year.

There are three values in South Africa that can be applied to rhino:
- a non-consumptive value (as above);
- a consumptive value, derived from a legal hunt; and
- one described by the Saaymans as 'existence value' (see below)

In the Saaymans' words: 'The existence value is what people assign to a species simply because they derive value from knowing these species are safe for future generations to enjoy.' Therefore this value is the most difficult to determine, since it is not captured or dealt with by one organisation or entity and it involves everyone (locals and foreigners) that assigns a value to the existence of an animal.

This important study reveals an aspect not generally taken into consideration, and when one adds the tens of millions in donations since this war commenced over one species, the figures are astonishing. In summary, according to the Saaymans:

> The total value of the rhino population in South Africa can be thought of as the sum of these three values and this lies between US$22.7 million and US$41.8 million annually. What we learn from this is there is much more to rhinos than just their horns. It is a very valuable animal that should be protected by all means possible.[4]

I would like to illustrate one private rhino owner's contribution in the 'non-consumptive' value of rhino, although rhino per se are but one component of the experience. This 3 000-hectare reserve is situated in the Waterberg of the Limpopo Province. There are two world-class lodges with a capacity of 40 beds. Horse riding is a principal attraction and the client base is largely from the UK/US. Occupancy amounts to some 6 000 bed nights per year or roughly an occupancy of 80%. General game including buffalo and white rhino can be seen in the reserve. The operation employs about 80 staff, the bulk of whom are from the local community. Rhinos are a key element in the visitors' experience and they are more than happy to pay the conservation levy that goes towards the security of these animals.

Tessa Baber, the owner of Ant Africa Safaris (a member of the Classic Africa Collection), is the founder of the Save the Waterberg Rhino (STWR), which promotes the conservation of all rhino in the 1 750 000-hectare Waterberg Biosphere. They are actively engaged in promoting awareness of rhino to the local youth, most of whom have never seen a rhino before or been anywhere near a game reserve. STWR is a non-profit organisation, formed a number of years ago after a series of poaching incidents in the area, with the aim of galvanising action on the part of rhino owners to support improved security for not only rhino but the community at large. Three large conservancies have been formed, which have benefitted greatly from this organisation's assistance. Forewarned is forearmed, and lessons have been learnt from as far afield as Kenya. To win this battle, the fight must be taken to the enemy and the enemy needs to know that if they enter these conservancies, they will be flagged down and followed.

The economic contribution of tourism, game farming and associated activities is considerable to the local communities, by way of job opportunities, training and educational investment in the youth, not least the support of local businesses. Conservation of rhino goes well beyond simply their protection – it extends into general crime prevention with active participation in support of the local police through the Community Police Forum (CPF) and local landowners.

This is but one example of the massive contribution that the private sector makes across South Africa, Botswana, Namibia, Swaziland and Zimbabwe as owners of rhinos or as custodians through non-consumptive use (tourism) and through their 'existence value'.

So is the rhino worth saving? The short answer is 'yes', but we need to change the perception that a dead rhino is worth more than a living one. Wildlife is the sovereign jurisdiction of a nation.

LEFT: An armed ranger poses with two patrol horses in a Waterberg reserve. Horses play a valuable role in various reserves in combating poaching incursions due to their ability to move over long distances with minimal disturbance. Photo: STWR.

BELOW: This photograph well illustrates the considerable cost of protecting a species such as we see here. To train a ranger to this level and maintain his presence in a given reserve is very expensive. Next time you are in a reserve with rhino or elephant and you notice there is a conservation levy, this is what you are contributing towards. Photo: STWR.

How we treat the environment and its inhabitants, apart from ourselves, is a reflection of the values of that country – or the absence thereof. Sadly, for much of the world's biodiversity, time is running out.

Kruger translocations – establishing new populations of black rhino

Prior to 1990 there were no black rhino on private land in South Africa – their conservation was strictly a national affair. The bulk of rhino were in the Zululand reserves of the southern subspecies, *Diceros bicornis minor*. A small population of the subspecies from East Africa, *michaeli*, had been translocated to Addo Elephant National Park in 1962 as a safeguard for the species. The last black rhino in the Orange Free State (Free State) was shot in 1842, and the last Cape rhino was shot in the Port Elizabeth area in 1853. Fortunately, both the black and white rhino were declared 'Royal Game' in 1890 in Zululand and only the governor could give permission for them to be hunted. By 1895 the species was accorded absolute protection. Then strangely in 1897 the proclamation was repealed and the species placed in a different schedule – upon paying a licence fee of the princely sum of the equivalent of R20 per rhino, you could hunt them as long as you took down no more than two animals each. Fortunately both Hluhluwe and Imfolozi were proclaimed the same year, thus in the nick of time providing absolute protection to the species.

When the Kruger National Park was proclaimed in 1926, only four or five black rhino remained. The last black rhino, a cow, was seen in the Kruger National Park in 1936 and a programme of reintroduction had been instigated by the two Parks Boards (National Parks of South Africa and the Natal Parks Board). It was in fact a very sensible decision for Kruger, as by virtue of its size it was a prime choice for the species introduction. It is necessary to acknowledge the role played by the people involved as it has proved to be the best safeguard for the species in South Africa.

The first translocation of 20 black rhino to Kruger took place in 1971 from Hluhluwe Game Reserve, followed by a further group of 12 from Rhodesia (Zimbabwe) in 1972. That year I was to meet Peter Hitchins of the Natal Parks Board for the first time and, according to him, by 1975 there was a total of 439 black rhino within reserves in South Africa. By 1982, no less than 70 animals had been safely introduced into Kruger.[6]

The Phoenix was slowly rising from the ashes of the past mindless slaughter.

ABOVE: An airborne Bell Jet Ranger helicopter on a rhino capture operation deep in the Zululand bush during the relocation of black rhino to the Kruger National Park in the 1990s. Photo: Clive Walker.

OPPOSITE TOP LEFT: A black rhino released into the Kruger National Park from one of the then Natal Parks Board reserves. Photo: Herman Potgieter

OPPOSITE TOP RIGHT AND BOTTOM: The capture of a large female black rhino who had gone down in extremely dense bush and required to be 'walked' some 100 metres to the transport vehicle. Risk is attached to both the rhino and rhino handlers and is not for the faint-hearted in these circumstances. A vet involved in the operation had two fingers crushed while the rhino entered the container. Photo: Clive Walker.

TOP: A makeshift capture boma site in the first operation to bring the black rhino back to the Kruger National Park in 1971. Photo: Peter Hitchins.

BOTTOM: The Natal Parks Board team who were responsible for the first introduction of black rhino to the Kruger National Park (KNP), which was last seen in 1936. LEFT TO RIGHT: David Wearne, Stewart Herd, Mike Keep, Dr Tol Pienaar (director of the KNP), Peter Hitchins, Dirk Swart and Ken Rochat. Photo: Peter Hitchins.

Peter Hitchins, technical officer, together with Ken Rochat, chief capture officer of the then Natal Parks Board, were directly involved in the very first translocations to Kruger in 1971 and they were both part of the team evaluating private properties in 1989. Hitchins worked for the Natal Parks Board for close on 13 years and was to devote a great portion of his life to the conservation of the species.

Since 2014 Kruger has been selling and moving a large body of white rhino out of the park. They have also built a 'Berlin Wall' – an intensive protection zone (IPZ) – in an undisclosed area within the park with generous funding. This has enabled the park authorities to move additional rhino to a safer environment.

Black rhino range-expansion programme of the WWF

This project was established in 2003 by Dr Jacques Flamand,[7] a former veterinarian of the Natal Parks. Funded by the World Wide Fund for Nature (WWF),[8] it has established no less than 160 black rhino since that date, representing 10 new populations on more than 220 000 hectares of land in South Africa. For security reasons, these respective reserves have not been identified – they are a combination of state, private and community involvement that holds great promise.

Having worked on the project since its inception, Dr Flamand reports that they have partnered with fantastic organisations over the years, including Ezemvelo KZN Wildlife, Eastern Cape Parks and Tourism Agency, and many private and community landowners. Partnerships make it possible to do things that cannot be done alone. So far all the projects are in South Africa, but they are looking forward to working with equally passionate people in southern Africa in order to build up their black rhino populations.

Dr Flamand is one example of the high calibre of people within southern Africa, both private and state, who have been at the forefront of rhino conservation for decades – especially in the early days in Zululand and Zimbabwe when black rhino were captured on foot in dense, tsetse fly- and malaria-infested bush, with temperatures reaching 40 degrees. They often worked with antiquated vehicles with no budget for the construction of boma (holding pens) or anything else, and where rhino were manhandled on top of mattresses onto the backs of trucks. They could never have achieved anything without the game rangers and their field staff who did the heavy lifting in these operations, often in dangerous situations involving accidents, as well as the dangerous presence of lion, buffalo and elephant. Today it is very much easier with crane-fitted trucks, helicopters, refined drugs, good radio communication and excellent facilities – a heavy-lifting helicopter can pluck the rhino off the ground by all four feet using a long, fibre cable and fly it directly to the boma.

With so much exposure of dead and dying rhino images these days, it is so easy to forget those men and women out there playing such vital roles together with the anti-poaching units and rangers guarding rhino 24/7 – they are all owed a debt of gratitude.

Sanctuaries and safety ... a costly exercise

While preparing this manuscript I was fortunate to be able to accompany Anton to the Rhino Pride Foundation. The founder and chair of this sanctuary is Jana Pretorius, a dedicated and committed veterinarian. Anton wanted to check on the condition of two young white rhino, aged 8 and 12 months, that had become separated from their mothers in a capture operation after purchase from a neighbour who was divesting in rhino conservation. He had lost a black rhino and three white ones in less than a week to poaching.

Another committed elephant and rhino rehabilitator in Africa is Karen Trendler, whose pioneering work on both species is legendary. She assisted my wife, Conita, back in the '90s with vital information on rearing black rhino calves. Karen today works at the Thula Thula Rhino Orphanage in KwaZulu-Natal.

Petronel Nieuwoudt is another tireless worker who founded Care for the Wild Rhino Sanctuary in Mpumalanga. She is one of the few people worldwide who has specialised in the care of orphaned and injured rhinos, and her passion is truly inspiring.

In the saving and capture of these rhinos, the role of the veterinarian is extremely vital – they are often the ones who come face to face with the bloody handiwork of the poacher and then have to do their utmost to rescue the calves before passing them on. All these dedicated individuals and their staff are more often the second or third responders after a rhino killing where there may be badly wounded animals or calves that may have been orphaned, dehydrated, terrified or traumatised. A baby rhino is subjected to the atrocious killing and decapitation of its mother, as well as the stench of drying blood, buzzing flies and decaying flesh. The calf, apart from being terrified, can be extremely aggressive and has to be rapidly subdued, examined and hydrated before removal from the crime scene. Flown by helicopter or vehicle, it will be quickly moved to these sanctuaries – and thus begins the costly and lengthy programme of recovery. Orphanage centres have had to develop as a consequence of

LEFT: Well-known veterinarian Dr Pierre Bester of the Waterberg in Limpopo preparing an immobilising dart. Veterinarians and the rhino capture teams they work with are critical to the management of rhino. Photo: Lapalala Wilderness/Dana Allen.

FOLLOWING PAGE: A heavy-lifting four-engine transporter of the Botswana Defence Force arrives at a remote airfield in the Okavango with a consignment of rare black rhino as part of the reintroduction programme. Photo: Dana Allen/Wilderness Safaris.

the onslaught of the country's rhino.

These centres have to be, or perhaps *should* be, under very high camera and electronic surveillance with armed guards 24/7. The recent assault and killing of two calves at the Thula Thula Rhino Orphanage is a stark reminder of the brazen behaviour of these criminals. Poachers were also reported by *Sky News UK* on 7 March 2017 as having gained access to a Paris zoo where they shot a white rhino three times in the head and then chain-sawed off one the horns before being disturbed. All this is the result of this mindless, bloody war.

The cost of all this capture, care and rehabilitation of these baby rhinos is enormous. Before weaning, a calf can consume up to R80 000 worth of milk in a year. The process involved in bringing the animal to adulthood is time consuming and very costly. For the orphans the story does not end there for they will eventually need to be restored to their former reserve or to be sent to an IPZ – that, too, is costly and potentially dangerous.

If the world is seriously concerned about the fate of the rhino and wants to contribute, then the responsible move is to push for the establishment of a 'Global Rhino Fund' to assist Africa.

'We are who we want to be, and we wanna be rhino.' This is the writing on the wall of Jana Pretorius's rhino IC unit at the Rhino Pride Foundation. Photo: Jana Pretorius.

Those of us who live and work with rhino in Africa make the plea to the world – African governments cannot do it alone, nor can the private rhino owner or the world's leading NGO movement ... we need your help and so does the rhino.

The work that has been undertaken since 2000

We have chosen four regions within southern Africa to illustrate the work that has been undertaken since the turn of the 21st century. They may not necessarily be considered Key Number 1 reserves as listed by the African Rhino Specialist Group (AfRSG) in terms of rhino numbers but, more than anything, they illustrate the new philosophy about what 'saving the rhino' is all about.

- Botswana – the Okavango Delta
- South West Africa (Namibia) – the desert-dwelling rhino
- KwaZulu-Natal – the iSimangaliso Wetland Park
- Limpopo – the Waterberg

Botswana – the Okavango Delta

The English 19th-century explorer, hunter and conservationist, Fredrick Courtney Selous, in 1879 observed there were still a few black rhino along the upper Chobe, north-west of the Savuti outlet. Bobby Wilmot, the legendary crocodile hunter, and his workers also reported seeing black rhino in the Okavango and on Chief's Island. By 1974 Dr Reay Smithers, in his work, *The Mammals of the southern African sub-region*, suggested that they had disappeared in Botswana. Occasional reports, however, suggested they may still have existed in the eastern Caprivi and northern Botswana as far south as Nxai Pan.

In 1988, Herman Potgieter and I were gathering material for a book on the Okavango Delta. Assisting us were Anton and our pilot, Andre Pelsor, as well as Lloyd Wilmot who knew the region better than most. Andre, Anton and I flew to Guma Lagoon on the western side of the Delta. Lloyd and Herman flew (in Lloyd's little four-seater Cessna 175) at low level to take photographs. The five of us would later join up and fly to Tsodilo Hills where there are the most amazing San rock art paintings, among which are numerous depictions of black rhino that I was anxious to record. To the north-west of Savute is a pan known as Tsantsara, which at certain times of the year is the only pan that still carries water in this vast wilderness. Lloyd, flying low in a wide circle towards the pan, was astonished to see below him two rhino running in the dry mopane woodland. Banking the plane around, he put the open-door side where Herman was stationed so he could photograph them – and sure enough he shot a magnificent black rhino cow and calf. At last there was living proof of the species' existence.

TOP: The Okavango Delta ranks as one of Africa's most stunning destinations and provides thousands with work opportunities within the tourism industry and a never-to-be-forgotten experience. Two locals punt across the Xaxaba water lily-covered lagoon at sunset. Photo: Clive Walker.

BOTTOM: Visitors to the Delta enjoy travelling on the numerous waterways by 'mekoro', the local term for a dugout canoe. In this image they are bird watching on one of the lagoons on the west side of the Moremi Game Reserve's, Chiefs island. Photo: Clive Walker.

TOP: Local children attending a Children in the Wilderness camp run by Wilderness Safaris as part of their environmental programme. Photo: Wilderness Safaris/Dana Allen.

BOTTOM: Red Lechwe antelope graze the edge of Mombo Camps flood plain. The organisation, Wilderness Safaris, has a high environmental ethic in their approach to nature-based tourism. Photo: Wilderness Safaris/Dana Allen.

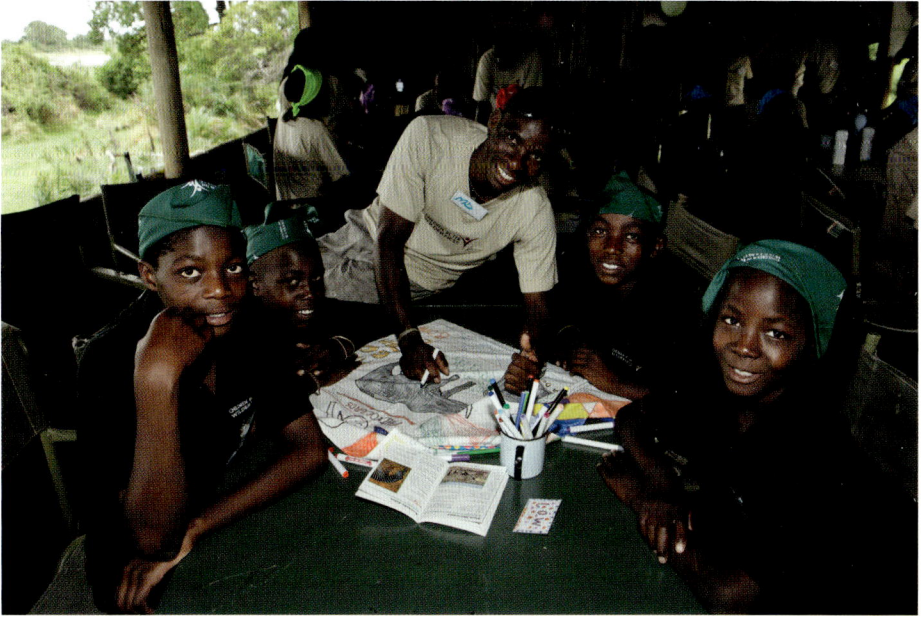

The news of the find was most encouraging and Peter Hitchins made it a priority that, as soon as funding was available, the Rhino and Elephant Foundation (REF) should make a serious attempt at a detailed aerial survey of northern Botswana to determine the status of the white rhino and hopefully reveal more black rhino. Botswana's white rhino were already extinct by the turn of the 19th century, and the then Natal Parks Board had undertaken the reintroduction of 90 of the species between 1974 and 1981, with funding from the Okavango Wildlife Society and the Frankfurt Zoological Society.

OPPOSITE TOP LEFT: Local guides smoking fish on the edge of a reed-covered lagoon. The local inhabitants west of the Boro River in the Delta make up a large component of the staff in the various nature-based tourism operations. Photo: Clive Walker.

OPPOSITE TOP RIGHT: This beautiful San (Bushman) image of three black rhino on a rock shelter can be found on an isolated mountain range in the north west of the Okavango River. Photo: Clive Walker.

OPPOSITE BOTTOM: This sublime, tranquil image requires no caption. Who would not want to be there? Photo: Wilderness Safaris/Dana Allen.

ABOVE: Future citizens of Botswana experiencing an environmental outing in the Okavango Delta. These youngsters represent the future custodians of this region's continued existence. We share the philosophy – leave no child behind. Photo: Wilderness Safaris/Dana Allen.

The long-awaited 15 000-km² rhino survey of northern Botswana finally got underway in September 1992, led by Peter Hitchins with Andre as lead pilot and Anton as the principal navigator. To ensure no problems were encountered, we had Johan Kotze as flight engineer, making sure we stayed airborne at all times. All being equal, Botswana's white rhino population should have naturally increased to some 240 animals, bar natural mortality since introduction.

Using two aircraft flying at approximately 15–20 metres above the ground, with the second aircraft 1 000 metres astern and 500 metres to starboard, the survey got underway from its base at Lloyd Wilmot's Camp in Savute.

Botswana today is blessed with a president, Ian Khama, who is passionate about conservation, something very rare in Africa, paving the way for an excellent relationship. We had the full involvement of the Department of Wildlife, the Ministry of Wildlife of Namibia and the Natal Parks Board whose personnel acted as observers. Dr Mike Knight, today the chairman of the International Union for Conservation of Nature (IUCN), the AfRSG and a pilot with considerable experience also came along. The survey could not have had a more complete body of experienced field members under one thatched roof.

We had two weeks of 6:30 am take-offs and 3½ hours flying each morning, with follow-up flying in the late afternoon, avoiding eagles and vultures. At the end, no black rhino were found, and only seven white rhino (three were subsequently poached!). To add to the horror of it all, a black rhino cow and her calf that we

A South African/Namibian team of pilots, scientists, game rangers and flight engineers, led by Peter Hitchins, centre with binoculars in 1992, which determined the number of the last remaining white rhino in Botswana. Co-author Anton Walker is seated on the aircraft wing while the author is on the extreme right. Photo: Clive Walker.

had photographed some years back were slaughtered in two separate instances, thus signalling the extinction of Botswana's black rhino. Fortunately the survey report enabled Anthony Hall-Martin, Director Special Services of South Africa's National Parks, and Peter Hitchins to request the assistance of the crack rhino capture team of the Natal Parks Board. They were to save the few remaining live rhino in Botswana and move them to the established Khama Rhino Sanctuary near Serowe.

The concept of a rhino sanctuary in Botswana was originally proposed by Peter Hitchins and initiated by the Chobe Wildlife Trust under the chairmanship of Jonathon Gibson, supported by the REF. The idea that it should be near Serowe was initiated by two Serowe businessmen, Ray Watson and Tony Ballantine, as a safe area for both species due to the serious situation prevailing in southern Africa. Serowe was a good choice for it had a nearby Botswana military base and was far enough from any border. More importantly, Serowe is the traditional centre of the Bangwangwato tribe whose head at the time was Ian Khama, Botswana's president, who also headed the military. He agreed to have his family name linked to the sanctuary.

The establishment of the Khama Rhino Sanctuary came in the nick of time with the generous support of WWF Hong Kong, the Chobe Wildlife Trust and the Kalahari Conservation Society, and is unique in Africa for it amounted to a wildlife sanctuary established by tribal people for tribal people. Working closely with the government's Department of Wildlife clearly illustrates the ability of NGOs to come together in a cooperative effort of this magnitude.

Botswana, in a hair's breadth, avoided seeing their white rhino become extinct twice in the same century.

Perhaps one of the best examples of private-sector and state cooperation commenced in 1999 in a combined operation with the Department of Wildlife and National Parks of Botswana, South Africa, Zimbabwe and the private Wilderness Safaris who had established some of the finest luxury, tented camp operations in the Okavango Delta.

The Okavango is an inland delta in the dry Kalahari sandveld of northern Botswana, in the district of Ngamiland. This district stretches from the Namibian border in the west to the boundary of the Chobe National Park in the east. It is bounded in the north by western and eastern Caprivi.

The word *ngami* comes from the Bayei word *ncama*, which means a floating mat of reeds. Within Ngamiland lies the Okavango Delta, whose 15 000 km^2 covers about 3% of Botswana's total land surface of 582 000 km^2. The waters that form the Delta originate in the Angolan Highlands to the north-west, less than 300 km from the Atlantic Ocean. Like the Nile River in Egypt, the Okavango sustains life in an inhospitable habitat. The region is essentially flat, with the exception of the Tsodilo

Hills, west of the village of Sepupa on the edge of the Okavango, and a series of hills (the Gcoha, Gubatshe and Chinamba) east of Savuti.

A vast treasure trove of San rock art occurs at Tsodilo Hills and the five of us (myself, Anton, Herman Potgieter, Andre Pelsor and Lloyd Wilmot) finally flew there in 1988. Of the many sites depicting black rhino, one shows a beautiful portrayal of two adult rhino and a calf. The present-day inhabitants west of the Boro are the Bayei and Humbukushu people. On the eastern panhandle where the Delta begins to fan out is the main Bayei village of Seronga (meaning 'whirlpool'), where their occupation may have commenced in the 18th century. This has been their world for some 300 years or more.

Wilderness Safaris,[9] in conjunction with the South African National Parks, Zimbabwe National Parks, and Botswana's Department of Wildlife and National Parks (DWNP), succeeded from 2003 onwards in returning the first of many translocations of not only the critically endangered black rhino into the region of the Okavango Delta, but also the white rhino. They have settled well into this vast landscape. July 2015 saw the last of eight translocations using a Hercules C130 transport aircraft, the largest transborder airlift of black rhino ever.

The area is bounded in the west by the Boro Channel, Moremi Game Reserve and the Linyanti region, and it is sufficiently far from settlements, although from past experience we know just how far poachers can penetrate a neighbouring country undetected. Botswana has gone to great lengths to place the best-trained anti-poaching units into undisclosed areas in question, with the support of the military. They remain supported by Wilderness Safaris, who have an outstanding track record when it comes to their operations anywhere in Africa. They also have a powerful conservation ethic, their staff welfare really matters, they have ongoing training, and an amazing programme of environmental education for local school children.

Botswana is one of Africa's great conservation destinations with spectacular wildlife, and is fully aware of the tourism potential in terms of the country's growth. Furthermore, they are a stable and democratic society, withstanding no nonsense when it comes to any form of criminal activity related to poaching their heritage. No one is under any illusion of the threats that rhino face – Botswana is no exception and it knows it must remain constantly vigil. There is a great deal at risk here as the region is not fenced, not to keep poachers out, but to keep the rhino secure. This necessitates very careful monitoring and crack anti-poaching units constantly alert.

The goodwill of surrounding communities will play a key role in the long-term success of this bold initiative.

South West Africa (Namibia) – the desert-dwelling rhino

Little is remembered of the pioneering translocations of the black rhino from what was formerly known as the Kaokoveld, known today as the Kunene Province. This vast area of more than 9 million hectares in the north-west of Namibia, running parallel to the famed Skeleton Coast up to the Kunene River and the border of Angola, was the subject of horrendous poaching of the desert-dwelling wildlife. This included rhino, elephant and giraffe, and we would have lost all three species if the situation had not been revealed by the Endangered Wildlife Trust (EWT) back in 1978.

Accounts of this may be read in Garth Owen-Smith's book, *An Arid Eden*, and the authors' work, *Rhino Keepers*. The last remaining black rhino of the subspecies *Diceros bicornis bicornis* were only to be found in low numbers in both Damaraland and Kaokoland, which made up the Kaokoveld – elsewhere they were extinct in South West Africa. Their timeous capture and removal to the Etosha National Park, largely undertaken by the official conservation agency led by the likes of the late Dr Hymie Eberdes, contributed considerably to their survival. Those remaining came close to extinction at the hands of poachers, which included members of the South African Defence Force operating within the then South West Africa.

Their certain extinction was averted with the assistance of organisations such as the EWT, Save the Rhino Trust, SAVE (an NPO based in New York), followed by the David Shepherd Foundation and today Save the Rhino Foundation, both based in the UK.

FOLLOWING SPREAD: The experience of viewing a solitary black rhino in this environment cannot be repeated anywhere else in Africa. These rare and endangered animals came very close to extinction in the 1980s and it is due in large part to many concerned, dedicated individuals and the commitment of various NGOs and the private sector that they still occur in this region. Photo: Wilderness Safaris/Dana Allen.

The recovery of the desert-dwelling rhino was due to the combined efforts of all these organisations. Success has been achieved through various community-based resource programmes, such as Wilderness Safaris who operate a number of high-end camps of which the Desert Rhino Camp actively promotes rhino-viewing. This may seem a contradiction in terms of previous comments about not identifying the rhino areas, but in this case the situation has been known for a very long period (as it has been in Etosha). Here rhino-viewing is a crucial element in the visitor experience, which of necessity requires high levels of surveillance.

In spite of the 'phoenix rising', and sadly in spite of all these successes, poaching of this subspecies has reared its head once again: 61 killed in 2014; 91 in 2015; and 63 in 2016. In total 215 black and white rhino have been killed over the past four years in Namibia (the number of elephants killed since 2013 amounted to 266). In fact, the slaughter goes back almost 10 years, although this is not generally acknowledged. Most, it would appear, occurred in the Etosha National Park.

According to the *Namibian Sun*: 'Nonetheless, poaching convictions have been legible and poaching suspects, including repeat offenders, have been routinely released on bail, often amid public protest.'[10]

This revelation has shaken Namibia conservation and illustrates the essential need to recognise that in vast, seemingly empty environments, the need for vigilance is paramount. This further illustrates the realisation of what it takes to protect this vast landscape with such a valuable animal and why they need our support.

Nowhere in Africa today can one witness these splendid animals in such environments. In spite of the upsurge in poaching, they represent a wonderful example of state, private-sector management, investment and community participation.

OPPOSITE TOP LEFT: The unique desert-dwelling OvaHimba people of northern Namibia are part of the living fabric of human life that inhabits this region. Photo: Clive Walker.

OPPOSITE TOP RIGHT: Elephant may also be found in this harsh environment and were heavily poached for their ivory in the '70s and '80s. They may be found in many localities today. Photo: Clive Walker.

OPPOSITE BOTTOM: At the end of a perfect day, there are a number of inspiring camps you can return to such as this lovely setting on the edge of an open desert plain. The object of these safari destinations is to provide the total experience. Photo: Wilderness Safaris/Dana Allen.

KwaZulu-Natal – the iSimangaliso Wetland Park

This park has been illustrated here because of its diverse range of landscapes, from the shores of the Indian Ocean, coastal dunes, forests, freshwater lake systems and swamps, to the inland bushveld regions. It is not a prime rhino reserve, although both species have been introduced here. The park is pivoted around the 80-kilometre long and 23-kilometre wide Lake St Lucia. This is comprised of three major lake systems, one of which has a fishing tradition over 700 years old and is one of the most important waterbird breeding areas in South Africa. The entire system represents an astonishing example of what state, communities and the private sector can achieve by coming together.

There have been long, hard-fought, bloody battles to save what was popularly known as Lake St Lucia, going back to the apartheid era led by the former Natal Parks Board. No other reserve in Africa can match this park in terms of its biodiversity and range of habitats. It is simply astonishing and it is not surprising it was accorded World Heritage Status in 1999. Today the park management falls under the control of Ezemvelo KZN Wildlife, a joint operation with iSimangaliso Wetland Park.

Not only is the park spectacularly beautiful, stretching over 220 kilometres of ocean front from Kosi Bay in the north on the Mozambique border to Maphelane in the south and across to the Mkuze Reserve in the west, but it is equally spectacular in terms of species diversity. There are 526 species of birds, 800 hippo, some 2 000 crocodiles, sharks, whales, porpoises, the world's largest marine leatherback turtle (*Dermochelys coriacea*), elephant, buffalo and both species of rhino, three major lake systems, and a 700-year-old fishing tradition.[11]

This 332 000-hectare park represents an excellent example of where the local people are central to the long-term wellbeing of a protected area. Trust is a key element here and it behoves the authorities to ensure that communities remain active participants and not just passive bystanders. The principal objective is to ensure communities benefit directly.

OPPOSITE TOP LEFT AND RIGHT: One of the great attractions of the Wetland Park is its amazing diversity of habitats and birds, of which there are 526 species. Photo: Clive Walker.

OPPOSITE BOTTOM: The park, which is a World Heritage Site, is home to crocodile, hippo, both species of rhino, elephant and buffalo. Photo: Clive Walker.

FOLLOWING SPREAD TOP AND BOTTOM: The magnificent, unspoilt coastline of the iSimangaliso Wetland Park comprises high dunes and stretches over 220 kilometres. The top image is of Mabibi North Beach and the lower image is of Bhangi Neck in the north of the park. Photo: George Hughes.

Limpopo – the Waterberg

The Waterberg straddles the Tropic of Capricorn, once home to both species of rhino, but most certainly hunted to extinction with the arrival of settlers, hunters and traders around 1850. The rhino was of course well known to the original San inhabitants. There are no less than four rock art sites that hold depictions of rhino in the spectacular caves and overhangs of the rugged northern escarpment. The San were followed by the iron-age farmers who arrived around 800 AD. They too had an interest in the rhino as revealed in the rare find of a small clay rhinoceros at the archaeological site of Melora. Melora Hill, a prominent landmark, lies at the centre of the impressive Lapalala Wilderness where the University of South Africa (UNISA) has worked since the late '80s. According to Booyens and Van der Ryst (2016): 'Two significant discoveries on Melora Saddle include a rare clay figurine of a rhinoceros and a pot burial. The African rhino, in particular the black rhino, served as a leadership symbol in traditional African society.' For more information on San rock art and other art forms, see the box at the end of this section.

The Waterberg is a vast, magnificent hinterland, which had gone unnoticed due to the difficulty of penetrating its interior through its rugged escarpments before the beginning of the early 20th century. When the settlers got a step in, the once-abundant wildlife vanished. It largely became overrun with poor landowners, who mostly lived off the veld, and land barons who acquired vast swathes of bushveld with a view to cattle farming and the possibility of mineral wealth. After the Anglo-

10mm

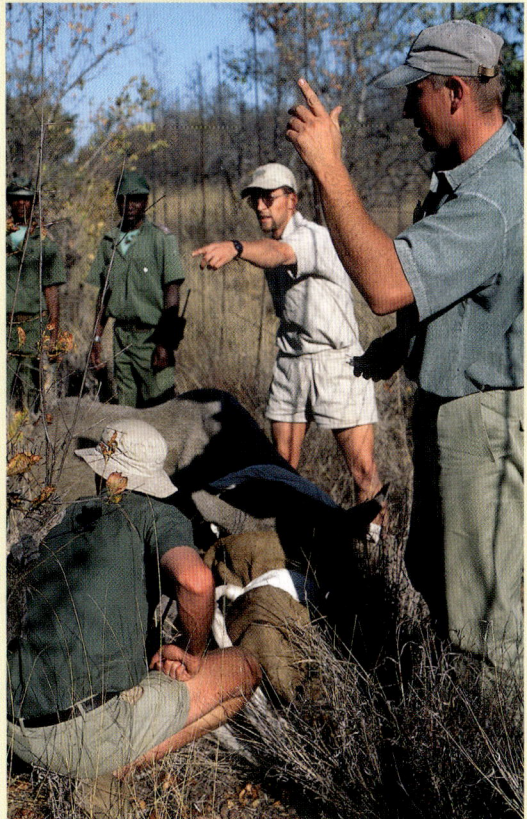

TOP: Fitting an ankle tracking collar to an immobilised white rhino's hind ankle in the Waterberg. Photo: Dana Allen.

RIGHT: Anton Walker directs operations during the capture of a white rhino. Rhino may be injured in fighting, requiring medical attention, or moved for management reasons. It is most important to monitor the wellbeing of rhino, especially on small properties. Photo: Clive Walker.

OPPOSITE: The small clay rhinoceros figurine found at the Melora site, circa 800 AD, in Lapalala Wilderness demonstrates that early people also had an interest these animals. Photo: UNISA Archaeology.

TOP: Children having the rare opportunity to view a young orphan black rhino up close. Photo: Clive Walker.

BOTTOM: A field ranger checks the condition of a black rhino whilst being held in a holding pen prior to release. Photo: Bruno Zanzottera.

Tourists come to Africa to see its wildlife and the rhino rates very high on their list of species to see. Photo: Clive Walker.

Boer War (1899–1902), the area fell back into obscurity and the once-vast herds of game were but memories in the minds of old men.

For the best part of the next 70 years, cattle, tobacco, maize and groundnuts occupied the time of most landowners, but the landscape was about to change with the advent of a new generation of landowner, the game farmer. In 1981 the Double R Game Ranch was acquired by Cape Town businessman, Dale Parker, adjacent to the Palala River covering 5 000 hectares, known as the Lapalala Wilderness. Dale, a visionary who recognised the value of wild country, set the stage for a massive transformation of the landscape. In those days, 90% was given over to agriculture – at the time of writing, this has reverted to 80% wild country with one national park, Marakele, and a large number of very impressive wildlife reserves and game farms. The National Park, combined with the 23 000-hectare Marakele Pty Ltd, measures some 60 000 hectares.

The Waterberg, which was once a tired and overgrazed cattle area, is today wild country with the return of the Big 5, elephant, buffalo, rhino (both species), lion, leopard, as well as hippo. By providing habit for these species, the whole spectrum of animal and plant life has been transformed. Not only has the biodiversity been transformed, but so has the human landscape in terms of employment, training, health care, education, business opportunities, skills transfer, security and the vital role that 'tourism' plays. Visitors want to see wildlife and the rhino is right up there

Environmental education of a country's youth is one of the best investments a country can make. Sadly, most African countries pay scant attention to this important issue, which has largely been left to NGOs. South Africa is fortunate in this regard, where corporations and private individuals play a major role in supporting various initiatives. Photo: Clive Walker.

on their score card, with many people travelling halfway around the world for this privilege. Game farming has been accused of causing job losses in agriculture – this is utter nonsense – the situation is quite the reverse.

It is necessary to be very mindful of talking in terms of rhino numbers, but it is common knowledge that the 1 750 000-hectare Waterberg Biosphere is home to both species of rhino and they are well adapted. All of this transformation has come at a cost since 2008 when a serious spike in poaching took place in South Africa. The private landowners have largely been on their own with no outside funding, but this has not prevented them from moving to save the rhino, generate jobs, create successful tourism, provide bursaries, set up health clinics, build craft projects and start 43 eco-school programmes. The most-celebrated environmental school in South Africa is based in the Lapalala Wilderness. No less than 80 000 school children, teachers and university students have passed through their doors since 1985.

In order to combat crime, there is close cooperation between the police and like-minded landowners; however, the Waterberg has not escaped the notice of poaching gangs. With the founding of Save the Waterberg Rhino (STWR), an NPO operating within the entire region, drastic action is being taken to combat rhino poaching. This is also about combating 'crime' in general, which affects everyone whether a rhino owner or not.

Cooperation is the essential key. Trust and learning from other initiatives, as well as the sharing of intelligence, is paramount.

ABOVE: Nothing will compare to encountering such an animal when on foot in the wilds of Zululand while on a walking trail. It has been described as the ultimate experience. They are very swift and extremely agile and a stout tree is your best option. Photo: Peter Hitchins.

RIGHT: For all the alarming reputation they have in the wild, it is amazing how soon they calm down in a holding pen and can be hand fed. There is a great deal about these animals we have yet to learn. Photo: Clive Walker

PRICELESS WORKS OF ART WILL NEVER REPLACE THE REAL THING

A rock art image of a black rhino on a reserve in the northern Waterberg mountain range of Limpopo. Photo: Clive Walker.

Rhino have been around for a very long time, we know this from fossil records, but we also know in more modern times from the evidence of human contact with rhino back at least 30 000 years to the cave art in France and Spain. Magnificent examples of rhino and many other creatures were brilliantly executed on these cave walls, leaving a lasting legacy of their contact. Were they simply just recordings of 'menu' animals or was there a far greater significance in their portrayal?

Imagine a world without rhino ... all we would have would be the 30 000-year-old cave paintings in Europe and the ones in rock shelters across southern Africa (such as in the Waterberg), as well as an extraordinary fossil record. There would also be a great deal of literature, photographs, museum pieces, wood, bronze and stone sculptors and depictions, dating back to the 16th century. In 1515 a German painter and printmaker, Albrecht Dürer, executed a woodcut of a rhino. The image was based on a description and sketch of an Indian rhinoceros that had arrived in Lisbon in 1515. Dürer never saw the actual rhinoceros, but it was the first living example seen in Europe since Roman times.

The 1515 woodcut of an Indian rhino by Albrecht Dürer. Probably the most famous depiction of a rhinoceros in the world. Photo: Rhino Resource Centre.

In the ancient past, the depictions were not meant as portrayal of art as we know it today, although we treasure them as such. Fortunately, there are numerous modern-day art depictions of rhinos by many distinguished artists from Africa, Europe and America who have enriched our world. In many instances they have helped the rhinos' cause, many donating handsomely to rhino conservation, while at the same time leaving us with examples of these magnificent creatures.

It is perfectly understandable to think of artists not only creating visions of beauty, but also to feel driven to give something back for the privilege of working in this field. Some of the well-known and celebrated artists are as follows:

A finely executed image of three rhino by the South African artist Alan Ainslie. Photo: Alan Ainslie.

A powerful acrylic painting of a pair of black rhino by the late Keith Joubert. Photo: FES Archive.

David Shepherd, the British-born artist, painted and raised funds for wildlife until he was well into his 80s. He was passionate about wildlife and wild places and made it his life's work, bringing joy to thousands through his art, books and lectures.

The late Paul Bosman, a South African who painted the elephants in the desert of Kaokoland, left a treasure trove of paintings, prints and publications, and generously donated hundreds of thousands of rand to this cause.

Bob Kuhn is a celebrated American animal painter.

Robert Bateman is a Canadian-born painter.

The late Keith Joubert was a generous and brilliant artist with a unique style.

Alan Ainslie, the Cape-based animal artist, has the distinction of being a painter and sculptor (whose first one-man exhibition opened in 1989). He is totally committed to the cause of conservation through his talent.

Keith Calder is a South African-born sculptor.

Kim Donaldson, with his outstanding diversity in medium, has his own art gallery in Franschhoek in the Cape.

Dylan Lewis has his brilliant life-size sculpture of a black rhinoceros gracing the entrance to Ezemvelo KZN Wildlife headquarters in Pietermaritzburg.

It will indeed be an appalling indictment if all we are left with is rock art, modern-day paintings and digital images of what the five remaining species of rhinoceros once looked like.

Priceless works of art, no matter how good, how ancient, how spiritual and uplifting, will never replace the real thing.

CHAPTER 4

Which way the rhino?

Good intentions, like some African rivers, are apt to run into sands of reports, committees, conferences and global strategies, which keep a lot of people busy but do not halt the poacher with his gun or poisoned arrow, the smuggler in his dhow, the importer with his fake documents. While people pass resolutions, rhinos die.

– Elspeth Huxley, Introduction to *Rhino Exploitation*

While people pass resolutions, rhinos die

In our research for this book we have been struck by the volume of literature that has been produced on the subject of rhinos. It is almost overwhelming — papers, reports, files, correspondence, press releases and cuttings. The Rhino Resource Centre (RRC) is a repository of all publications about all species of rhinos and is a service to everybody working with rhinos in zoos, museums, media, in aid of research, education and conservation. The total number of references in the database and collection of the RRC now stands at 21 550.[1] Having been involved with rhino for close on 40 years, we also have boxes and boxes of the stuff. How much has been forgotten or simply ignored is anyone's guess. Just going through it all has been a challenge. Now we must remind ourselves that there is an animal at the end of all the paperwork churned out over the years, and we must offer some judgements aimed at its survival.

In 1994 I was invited by the chairman, Dr Martin Brooks, to join the African Rhino Specialist Group (AfRSG) of the International Union for Conservation of Nature (IUCN) as a representative of the private rhino owners of South Africa. The AfRSG is one of a number of groups making up the Species Survival Commission of the IUCN. Its mission is to promote the long-term conservation of Africa's

ABOVE: South Africa played host to the CITES CoP17 conference which was held in Sandton, Gauteng in February 2016. Photo: WRSA.

OPPOSITE: Red Lechwe antelope of Botswana's Okavango Delta. Photo: Wilderness Safaris/Dana Allen.

PREVIOUS SPREAD: A desert-dwelling black rhino of the sub species *D.b. bicornis* from the Kunene Province in Namibia. Photo: Wilderness Safaris/Dana Allen.

Members attending the African Rhino Specialist Group meeting in Manyara, Tanzania in 2000. Photo: Walker Archive.

rhinos and, where necessary, the recovery of their populations to viable levels. It is charged with providing technical information and advice to both governments and non-governmental organisations, and with promoting and improving conservation activities to be carried out by these entities. One of the most vital functions has been to compile and maintain a database on the numbers of African rhino (see graph at the end of Chapter 2). The group comprises official representatives of the rhino range states and rhino specialists in the scientific, veterinary, research, field management and trade arenas. Trade issues have been an agenda item from the inception of the group and, given the current crisis, they warrant ever-closer attention. This has been studied and debated for more than 30 years, causing much division within the ranks of all concerned with rhino conservation.

Joining the AfRSG enabled me to meet and work with a wide spectrum of rhino experts from Africa and abroad for the following 14 years. It was a valuable and life-enriching experience and introduced me to many of the people in the field of rhino conservation. I am not a scientific specialist; rather I have worked with rhinos on the ground and in aerial surveys. They were entrusted to the care of my staff, and one of our objectives was to ensure that the private sector could play a meaningful role in rhino conservation (in particular the black rhino), a view that not everyone in the state conservation fraternity in South Africa shared at first. There were good reasons for doubt, for the private sector had not always demonstrated the highest standards and ethics, as I had found while director of the Endangered Wildlife Trust (EWT) and the Rhino and Elephant Foundation (REF). Today things are different.

In the first decades of the 21st century, we have come to realise that rhinos, in spite of having roamed our planet for millions of years, now live in very uncertain times. As discussed in the previous chapters, the rhino wars tailed off somewhat from 1994, when the continental population of black rhino had declined to about 2 400. Troubles were notable in Zambia, Zimbabwe, Botswana, Namibia, Swaziland and to a lesser degree South Africa. Mozambique had already seen the white rhino become extinct, and the same very nearly happened in Botswana. Least affected was South Africa as, although rhino poaching was always a feature in the Kruger National Park and the Zululand reserves, it remained at relatively low levels.

South Africa had an appalling track record in the decline of its wildlife in the 18th and 19th centuries. We witnessed the extinction of three large animal species and came close to exterminating both species of rhinos. Thanks to systematic conservation work since those early days, we can marvel at the fact that we now rank as the most advanced country in the world in the recovery of its wildlife and wildlife estate. The combined investments of the state and the private sector, especially in the area of wildlife ranching, turned the situation around. During the latter part of the 20th century, the rhino were able to struggle back from the brink.

If we look back to the decline of Africa's rhino since the 1970s, the conservation world certainly reacted to the threat: we set aside specially protected areas, conducted translocations to safer reserves, and involved private landowners; we saw training and equipping of rangers and the establishment of the Endangered Species Protection Unit (ESPU) as a division of the South African Police; and we saw the formation of the REF and the Private Rhino Owners Association (PROA) and security groups, with massive NGO support, media awareness campaigns and workshops to find ways to halt the killing.

In 1994 I was an introductory speaker at a symposium at the University of Pretoria on rhino as a game ranch animal, where I declared: 'We need a major public relations programme to highlight the situation and urgently promote new, bold and optimistic ideas for rhino conservation.' To be perfectly honest my words fell on deaf ears. South Africa during 1994 had other far more pressing issues to contend with. We certainly had *not* taken careful note of the outcome of the REF and Game Rangers Association workshop held in Skukuza in 1988, regarding security of rhino on the ground. As Elspeth Huxley so accurately observed back in 1982: 'While people pass resolutions, rhinos die.'

Fast forward to 2017, and we find a dark cloud over our country as a new menace has overtaken our rhino populations. Between 2008 and the end of 2015, poachers killed almost 6 000 rhinos, and in the process of law enforcement, 500 poachers paid with their lives. It's a clear case of winning the battle but losing the war.

Rhino deaths in South Africa from 2008 to the present:

- 2008 – 83 deaths
- 2009 – 122 deaths
- 2010 – 333 deaths
- 2011 – 448 deaths
- 2012 – 688 deaths
- 2013 – 1004 deaths
- 2014 – 1215 deaths
- 2015 – 1175 deaths
- 2016 – 1054 deaths
- 2017 January to June – 529

As is evident, there was a slight dip in 2015 and 2016, but obviously not enough. If we fail to halt this onslaught, we will witness the unravelling of all the excellent work of past decades. With hungry men in the front lines and greedy men in the back rooms, we are in a serious fight against a dangerous and criminal business.

Meanwhile, the price of rhino horn has escalated beyond belief. As we saw in Chapter 2, the average wholesale price for African rhino horn in Southeast Asia has shot from US$550 per kilogram in 1979 to US$750–1 000 in 1993[2] and now somewhere in the region of between US$35 000 and US$65 000 (±R865 000) per kilogram today.

The value of rhino horn today is so high that poachers are more than willing to take enormous risks. They are also well armed and highly skilful in tracking – I am not talking about starving park neighbours, but about blatant criminals. Kill one and others are waiting to step in. Today the picture is much more ominous than in past decades.

Rhinos displayed in the world's museums have not escaped attention either. They have attracted not armed poachers, but clever thieves who have found ways to penetrate these institutions and remove horns from mounted exhibits. The statistics are shocking and include thefts from our own South African museums. Another theft before 2008 is the world-record white rhino horn, 19 kilograms in weight and 1.6 metres in length, that was brazenly stolen from the Altyre family estate in Scotland. The rhino had been shot by Roualeyn Gordon-Cumming in 1847.

STOLEN RHINO HORN TIMELINE
Museum and auction house thefts since 2008

2008	South Africa (April): 120-year-old horn stolen.
2008	South Africa (April): unknown number of horns stolen from the Grahamstown Observatory Museum and the Grahamstown Museum.
2009	South Africa: two 19th-century horns stolen from Isiko Museums, Cape Town.
2009	USA: rhino skull stolen from cheque-cashing business; horns not recovered.
2009	UK: auctioneer pleaded guilty to stealing horn from a client.
2010	Germany: horn stolen from the Allwetterzoo Müenster.
2011	UK: mounted head of black rhino stolen from auctioneer.
2011	France: 10th-century horn stolen from Museum of Natural History, Rouen.
2011	Portugal: two 18th-century horns stolen from a university science museum.
2011	UK: rhino head stolen from the Haslemere Educational Museum.
2011	Germany: six horns stolen from Hamburg Zoological Museum.
2011	Germany: horn stolen from rhino exhibit, Museum of Natural Science; two horns stolen from a hunting museum.
2011	Italy: three horns stolen from Museum of Natural History, Florence.
2011	Belgium: attempt to steal a rhino head trophy from the Museum of Africa in Tervuren; rhino trophy head stolen from Museum of Natural Sciences in Brussels; two rhino horns stolen from African Museum, Namur.
2011	Czech Republic: rhino horns from Africa and Asia dating back to 1898 stolen from a Czech castle.
2011	France: 19th-century rhino head stolen from the Natural History Museum, Blois.
2011	UK: Victorian rhino horn stolen from the Ipswich Museum.
2011	France: rhino horn dating from 1935 stolen from the African Museum at l'ile d'Aix.

The timing of these thefts appears to follow a distinct pattern suggesting a syndicate operation.[3]

Investigation into the use of rhino horn

To backtrack to the 1980s for some perspective, Lee Talbot, the 1980–82 Director-General of the IUCN, wrote in his preface to Dr Esmond Bradley Martin's 1983 book *Rhino Exploitation*: 'A threat to a species or an area was perceived and conservationists reacted to the threat. Consequently, reactive conservation focuses on the effects, not the cause, therefore it usually treats the symptoms, not the basic illness; it emphasises cure, not prevention.' Those words written more than 30 years ago have even more resonance now than they did then.[4]

Bradley Martin's study, which commenced in 1978, mostly funded by the World Wildlife Fund (WWF) and IUCN, was to look into the question of the trade in rhino products, a practice that has gone on in China and Southeast Asia for thousands of years, as well as to get an understanding of beliefs about rhino horn in traditional medicine. He revealed that its use as an aphrodisiac was largely a myth; rather it was used as a remedy to relieve a whole string of ailments, from fever and headaches to arthritis.

WWF's desire was to deal with the cause of the problem through a campaign to stop the rhino horn trade. From October 1982 to February 1983, Bradley Martin visited 10 Asian countries: 'To discourage pharmaceutical wholesalers from further

Dr Esmond Bradley Martin, leading rhino horn and ivory trade specialist and member of the IUCN AfRSG. Photo: Michael Gunther.

dealing in rhino products, and to explain to practitioners of Traditional Chinese Medicine [TCM] why they should no longer prescribe rhino drugs, and to publicise in the mass media the plight of the rhino in Africa as well as in Asia, so that consumers would be more willing to use substitutes.'[5]

Bradley Martin travelled widely – few could have equalled his tenacity in uncovering the facts surrounding the use of rhino horn, from the Arabian states to virtually every country in Southeast Asia. He is considered the world's leading authority on the international trade in rhino products and has served on the IUCN's AfRSG from the 1980s. As members of the group, Bradley Martin and I travelled to many rhino meetings over the years, and he never ceased to amaze me in his ability to gather information. The group is made up of a diverse array of personalities whose collective knowledge made a huge contribution to our understanding of the situation of Africa's rhino.

It's all very well to say we are dealing only with the effects and not the cause of the problem, but what choice do we have? Those on the ground responsible for rhino in South Africa at the moment have to deal with the physical threat to the animals.

We are fighting fire with fire, and we appear to be losing. The carnage is an appalling indictment of our efforts so far.

Costs of protection

In a 1988 paper with reference to the 16 000-km^2 range of Zambia's Luangwa Valley, Prof. Nigel Leader-Williams and SD Albon calculated that in order to achieve a zero decline of rhinos, spending should have been US$230 per km^2 per year. The government was in fact spending only US$11 km^2 per year.[6]

The cost of protecting rhino today is simply staggering. As we saw in Chapter 2, the amount suggested by Tony Conway to protect rhino adequately in 2015 was US$4 426 per km^2 (at the time the exchange rate was around R12 to the dollar). This figure was calculated for a state-owned reserve of less than 1000 km^2 and the projections differ for larger reserves, with the exchange rate now nearer to R15 to the dollar at the time of writing.

TOP: Co-author Anton Walker and a capture team manoeuvring an immobilised large white rhino bull in the direction of the recovery vehicle. Photo: Clive Walker.

BOTTOM: Dr Pete Morkel, a veterinarian, removing a horn using a chain saw. Providing precautions are taken, the rhino suffers no ill effects and the horn will regrow at the rate of around 8 cm per annum. Photo: REF Walker Archive.

- Reserves smaller than 1 000 km^2
  - recommend one ranger per 10 km^2
  - costs R50 218 per km^2 per year
- Reserves larger than 1 000 km^2
  - recommend one ranger per 15–30 km^2
  - costs between R16 739 and R33 479 per km^2 per year[7]

At the lower cost of R16 737 per km^2, protecting rhino in the 20 000-km^2 area of the Kruger National Park could cost almost R350 million a year. The cost of securing rhino in South Africa in all the state-owned protected area systems has been estimated at R0.87 to R1.29 billion. Where in the world is that kind of funding going to come from? The total budget for South Africa's Department of Environmental Affairs (DEA) for 2015/2016 was R6 billion. Clearly one sixth of it cannot go into rhino protection.[8] These figures do not even include all the actual requirements of the ongoing battle, such as helicopters, fixed-wing aircraft and pilots, fuel, specialised equipment, drones, radio communications, and a command base and staff. Tracker dogs can cost R100 000 each to train, and staff need replacement vehicles and updated weaponry.

Park mandates are about protecting biodiversity, first and foremost. Sadly, most governments in Africa treat the wildlife estate as the 'Cinderella' department and provide inadequate funding for it to function properly. The NGO network has arisen to try to address the shortfall. In a 2010 article, Dr Crispian Olver (who was the Director-General of South Africa's Department of Environmental Affairs and Tourism from 1999–2005) presented a review of the effectiveness of the government conservation system. The report pointed out that there are 15 different official conservation management agencies in South Africa, and it went on to say that out of the 15, only five management authorities were performing adequately to well, and even those were showing signs of distress.[9]

Much of the shortfall in performance hinges on budget troubles, with the present government reducing the budgets of these agencies. In the case of Ezemvelo KZN Wildlife, the 2016 budget was only R143 million. Where budgets are swallowed up by salaries and barely cover these, let alone equipment or special projects, we surely have a prescription for disaster. A further sensitive issue largely overlooked has been 'the transformation of the civil service coupled with declining budgets, which led to many skilled and senior conservationists taking retrenchment packages, causing a skills shortage and reduced effectiveness of some provincial nature conservation departments'.[10]

So is the government even trying to take the matter seriously at the highest

levels? The state is more than aware of the costs, having been in the thick of this since 2008. Staff and budget constraints notwithstanding, efforts have been made to deal with the threat on the ground. The struggle to contain rhino poaching ultimately led to the DEA minister appointing a highly experienced, retired military officer, General Johan Jooste, as Officer Commanding Special Projects in January 2013. Initially he was to convert the ranger corps into an anti-poaching unit, and in the process he played a key role in formulating and implementing the current multi-faceted strategy in the Kruger National Park. Given the enormous pressure of ongoing incursions into Kruger, expecting someone without a military background to confront the poaching had become unrealistic.

At the beginning of 2016 General Jooste was appointed as Head of Special Projects at SANParks head office in Pretoria. From there he has gone on to establish a Wildlife Crime and Corruption Combatting Centre for all the SANParks reserves. Credit is due the state in dealing with this crisis by making a determined effort at transformation designed to bring the field rangers up to a stronger level of capability for dealing with the slaughter of Kruger's rhinos.

On 1 November 2015, SANParks appointed Xolani Nicholus Funda as the new chief ranger, with responsibilities for effectively managing the whole anti-poaching operations in the Kruger National Park. Kruger's managing executive, Mr Glenn Phillips said,

With communities bordering the national parks playing a major role in the fight against wildlife crime, Funda's return to the organisation came at the right time as his experience and knowledge of conservation expands to community beneficiary issues, which also have direct effects on the environment. As someone who worked as a ranger in his early career and has continued to have an impact on conservation efforts, we have faith in Mr Funda's abilities to address the ongoing challenges in conservation.[11]

OPPOSITE AND ABOVE: The Natal Parks Board pioneered the chemical capture and translocation of both species of African rhino in the Zululand reserves in the 1960s and led the way in the reintroduction of the species across southern Africa. Photo opposite: Clive Walker. Photo above: Shaen Adey.

The survival of the southern white rhino was entirely due to the foresight and timeous action taken in 1895 when the white and black rhino were declared 'royal game' in the reserves of Zululand. Photo: Clive Walker.

We, as authors, remain unconvinced that a park the size of Kruger, given its location, can adequately and indefinitely sustain the cost of defending attacks on its rhino population, let alone an upsurge in the killing of elephant as stated by Minister Edna Molewa in a press statement on 24 July 2017.

The question of *community beneficiary issues* in the short term also remains doubtful as stated by the authors in an earlier chapter.

We need to ask private rhino owners the same kinds of questions about security and effectiveness. Security and monitoring were probably close to zero on some properties that have lost rhino to poachers. As noted by the PROA chair Pelham Jones in Chapter 2, citing a DEA survey, by mid-2015 more than 1 000 rhino had been poached on private property. We believe a dramatic shift has taken place between conservation and ranching. The majority of owners have gone into rhino ranching, as evidenced by a market largely driven by the sale of surplus animals at auction, where the price is determined by trophy hunters.[12]

The proportion of the world's population of 15 000 white rhino that were held by private rhino owners at the end of 2005 was 21.1%. Today, according to Pelham Jones, that figure is 33% for white rhino and 28% for black rhino, which translates into more than 6 200 animals.[13] By 2009 the AfRSG and the wildlife trade monitoring network TRAFFIC were clearly aware of the increase in poaching from

2008. Red lights were clearly flashing, and both provincial authorities and private rhino owners must have been aware of the impending threats.

Sadly, the private sector as a whole paid scant attention to the lessons of the past, never believing the problem would affect them. But as earlier described, South Africa now faces new challenges: a massive surge in Asian expansion into Africa; a human population approaching 57 million; an ongoing influx of people from Zimbabwe and Mozambique, some with weapons experience; and escalating crime and a judiciary under considerable pressure. Furthermore, a new, far more sophisticated poacher has emerged, one who uses helicopters, drugs, dart guns and cellphones and is well acquainted with professional crime syndicates.

Rhino conservation comes with heavy risks. For the private rhino owner, the killing of one rhino is not only a major financial loss, it is also a personal loss in terms of stress and the realisation that rhino can no longer be left without intensive and perpetual protection. It is not surprising that the number who have given up ownership of the species has risen. The cost of this protection is prohibitive, and it is a dangerous business, with owners today needing to hire security organisations with armed rangers to protect their field staff and their animals. With regard to this, Pelham Jones commented:

> From independent survey data as well as PROA records, we identified that there were historically about 400 private reserves with rhino, but in 2015 this figure had dropped by some 70 reserves down to 330 (we believe that the figure of 330 has dropped further since 2015, but do not have data to confirm an exact number). Certain of these properties had all their rhino poached, others had some poached and the balance were sold. We estimate a habitat or range loss of about 200 000 hectares as a result.[14]

The poaching surge has galvanised owners into action to protect their interests. According to Pelham Jones, the conservative calculation of the financial loss of animals killed on private reserves since 2008 is US$30 million [±R400 million] and the annual cost of protection today of private rhino alone is estimated at US$25million [±R333 million].[15]

Rhino custodians

We have three types of custodians of rhino in South Africa that all make a valuable contribution to the species, but each group does so for entirely different reasons:

- The state agencies
- The conservationist landowners who are concerned with biodiversity conservation, which includes tourism and education based on sound landscape management. Their prime objective is not breeding and selling wildlife.
- The game ranchers who breed wild game primarily for the sake of making a profit.

In the forefront and leading the charge is Wildlife Ranching SA with Pelham Jones and his colleagues of the PROA working tirelessly.

[They have] established an excellent working relationship with a number of authorities directly involved in the rhino poaching saga. These include the Hawks, National Prosecuting Authority (NPA), the DEA at national and provincial level, SANParks, and in particular the National Wildlife Crime Reaction Unit (NWCRU). This interaction covers a wide spectrum of activities from investigations to providing information, and calling for assistance on behalf of rhino owners.[16]

The PROA works closely with a wide range of organisations and helps coordinate and implement projects in rhino preservation, while at the same time serving on a number of NGO committees. These include the Endangered Wildlife Trust (EWT), WWF, Stop Rhino Poaching, the SADC Rhino Management Group (RMG) and TRAFFIC SA. The liaison with the last two associations is of great importance.

Does the PROA have a vested interest? Of course they do.

The constitution of the PROA describes the need to protect and conserve the species. The PROA as an accredited NGO and NPO and is a member of various working groups.

Losing rhino is a financial nightmare for many reasons. Poaching brings dangerous and serious crime, involves trans-border violations, ties down state institutions, and is an embarrassment to the country at numerous levels, not least the DEA. It involves the worst of international crime syndicates, implicating countries far from our shores

Elise Daffue, director of the NGO Stop Rhino Poaching, has been hugely instrumental in providing vitally needed equipment to the official conservation agencies across South Africa. These NGOs play a critical role in the ongoing crisis. Photo: Chris Serfontein.

but to which we are now closely allied. Does anyone believe for one moment that South Africa is going to demand that China sets an example and conquers the illegal trade in rhino horn? Why would they when the trade between South Africa and China has developed so rapidly with China investing nearly US$6 billion (setting up more than 80 companies) in South Africa since 1998?[17]

Many high-profile South African rhino NGOs and corporations have responded. The dedicated members of the Game Rangers Association of Africa and the organisation itself are at the coal face, an indispensible element for winning the battle and the war. They need our support more than ever. It is hugely encouraging to note the financial support from many of the world's leading rhino NGOs, which recognise this need where the field force of official conservation agencies is increasingly hampered by severe budget constraints. There have been reports of bogus NGOs cashing in on the crisis, but our experience is that the principal ones play a critical role in support of rhino conservation, especially the Endangered Wildlife Trust, Save the Rhino International, the David Shepherd Wildlife Foundation, International Rhino Foundation, StopRhinoPoaching, Save the Waterberg Rhino, the Game Rangers Association Africa and TUSK (UK).

Much of the effort by these organisations has been centred on the training of field staff, providing vehicles, sniffer and tracker dogs, and specialised equipment to combat the threat.

Elise Daffue of the NGO Stop Rhino Poaching addressing a conference group on the ongoing rhino crisis. Photo: Chris Serfontein.

The world is not likely to put up the funding indefinitely, although the amounts to date are impressive, they still fall far short of the needs. The private rhino owners – of whom so much is expected because they are not bound by bureaucracy or the ills that beset government – make a contribution vital to the long-term survival of both rhino species, but they cannot carry the burden alone.

Seeking new solutions in the battle for the rhino

What is needed now, more than ever in our history, is for the state and the private sector to demonstrate urgently to the country and the world that we can conquer this scourge. Dr Michael Knight, chairman of the AfRSG, has the following advice:

[We need] an improvement in the underlying governance of our conservation estate and law enforcement establishments. This requires us to get on top of poaching that is currently killing just over three rhino a day. There have been improvements in reducing poaching in the KNP of late, which is very welcome. In addition, we need to clamp down on syndicates that are trafficking and selling the horn – and that is happening too slowly. This can only be achieved through a whole government response, together with civil society.[18]

One can understand, then, that a strong body of opinion exists within the conservation world in South Africa of very highly respected individuals who seriously believe that the only long-term, sustainable solution in saving the rhino is to lift the ban on trading in rhino horn.

These individuals are not owners of rhino and have no invested interest but nevertheless have a vast wealth of experience when it comes to understanding conservation needs on the ground.

The pro-trade lobby who own or manage rhino have not done enough, in our opinion, to demonstrate that a legal trade is not just about making money. This impression may well exist because rhino owners have different objectives. One group may well be perceived as investing in 'rhino' to make profits by live sales, hunting and potentially harvesting horn. The second important group conserve rhino for 'species' conservation, education, awareness and tourism. For them the conservation of the species is the ultimate objective. They also acquire 'horn' via mortality factors. This group include the private sector and the state-run reserves. Most I would imagine would sell 'horn' if it were legal but this would not be the primary objective.

Unfortunately the perception continues to exist both nationally and inter-nationally that any form of consumptive use is the principal objective and the pro-trade lobby need to accept that perhaps they have not done enough to dispel this persistent notion. A far more positive note needs to be projected.

Firstly, let us repeat, the cost to keep rhino for any reason is prohibitively high, almost too high given the number who have abandoned the rhino. It is our desire to illustrate through the pages of this book that we cannot afford to have any more owners abandon their rhino and to give the proponents of trade the opportunity of stating their case in the face of critics who are not offering any alternatives.

The anti-trade lobby are going to point out that we completely ignore the far more threatened and endangered three Asian species of rhino. What they overlook is that if the threat to Africa's rhino is reduced by a legal trade, greater resources from the International NGO movement could be more fully applied to these species who everyone recognises are far more vulnerable. There are other issues concerning the survival of these three species that require a separate debate. Are these countries' governments doing enough themselves?

We are not professing for one moment that we are qualified to address the complexities of trade but rather seek to create further dialogue through the pages of this book that the time of endless discussion is over. Sensible people would at least sit down to debate a way forward.

FOLLOWING SPREAD: A stunning image of a young black rhino somewhere in the Okavango Delta. Photo: Wilderness Safaris/Dana Allen.

Why do we believe a legal trade in rhino could save the rhino?

By providing a well-regulated and controlled supply of rhino horn to the market, compliant with national and international legislation, with transparent control measures to prevent 'blood horns' from entering the legal market, as stated by Pelham Jones of the Private Rhino Owners Association (PROA), the following scenario may well present a solid reason why all of us concerned with the rhinos' long-term survival can be bold enough to subscribe to.

It is high time we simplified the matter of why we believe a legal trade in rhino horn could turn the tide against poaching. Polarised debate between pro- and anti-trade conservationists sadly detract from our primary responsibility to save the species:

- To acquire the horn, it's not necessary to kill the animal, unlike with elephant ivory.
- Since there has always been a demand for horn in South East Asian culture, why not accept this and endeavour to meet the demand rather than block it. Bans and prohibitions have not proven successful in reducing poaching levels, but as an unintended consequence have created a vast illegal and transnational trade that benefits criminals and brings nothing back to aid conservation.
- By meeting the demands of legal trade, you reduce the risk of acquiring it illegally and reduce poaching levels on wild populations.
- A legal trade will reduce the law-enforcement burden, the impact of people being killed, the cost of the legal process to bring poachers to trial and jail, the impact on the families of anti-poaching members as well as that of the poachers.
- A legal trade will reduce the massive cost of protection to acceptable levels by selling from existing stock piles of horn held by national, provincial and private reserves.
- It will free up state- and private-sector funding for other vitally needed conservation work.
- It will vastly reduce the stress associated with high-level crime and its collateral damage on innocent lives.
- Trade in rhino horn can help create a conservation incentive. Currently we are experiencing a reduction in rhino range to poaching losses and related security costs. Twenty-three of an original 33 range states have lost all their rhino.
- It is argued that a legal trade has the potential to make rhino the most valuable and accordingly most protected animal in Africa.

The rhino's fate is in our hands right now. We can resist and go back to the same old practices of endless workshops and meetings and pass resolutions – rhinos will continue to die – or we can take bold, new steps, even if they are un-palatable, in our efforts to win this battle and this war.

Where are we today in this debate?

As long ago as 1999, AfRSG members Dr Richard Emslie and Martin Brooks observed:

> It is a simple but undeniable fact that if there was no demand for rhino horn, there would be little or no rhino poaching. Controlling the illegal supply of horn through anti-poaching measures is a very expensive strategy, and its long-term effectiveness is threatened by declining budgets. It is important to discover what drives the rhino horn trade, and examine the potential for reducing illegal demand.[19]

Eighteen years on, in 2017, we know what is driving the demand, but we are still examining the potential for reducing the illegal demand. As we have read earlier, rhino horn has been sought in ancient and modern times for medicinal and ornamental reasons, as an ingredient in TCM and for the manufacture of handles for highly prized ceremonial daggers worn by men in some Middle Eastern countries. Historically, horn was used for drinking goblets and bowls, and hide was used in the manufacture of war shields in northern Africa and China, as well as in the manufacture of body armour. As described in Chapter 7, other rhino parts have also been used extensively. Today TCM is still widely used throughout China and in other countries, but the dynamics have changed with a more sinister activity – its use as an investment and a status symbol.

We believe it is naïve to think that legislation or demand reduction will halt the killing of rhino in today's world. The value of rhino horn is colossal and the upkeep of the live animal is prohibitive. It is simply not sustainable in the long run in a continent bedevilled by poverty and corruption. The private rhino owner aside, where is the long-term funding going to come from in protecting state reserve rhinos? The private rhino owner has to fund him- or herself and, as reported by Pelham Jones, a number of them have simply given up.

It is therefore incumbent on us to question those who oppose the lifting of the

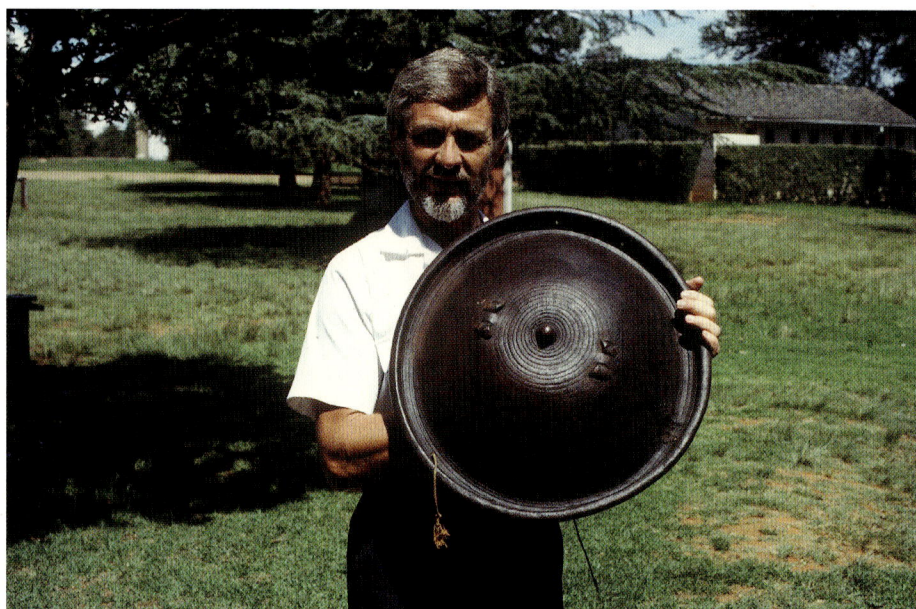

Clive Walker with an antique rhino hide shield from Ethiopia. Photo: Jane Zimmerman.

ban on the trade in rhino horn to consider the following: those dying in this crisis; the staggering cost in security; the associated stress and threats on people's lives; the tying up of state and private sector legal costs; increasing criminal elements; the stress on an already overstrained criminal justice system; and the diversion of funding from other important biodiversity conservation work.

Demand reduction and stricter legislation is the counter argument, along with the inability to sustain the Asian demand for horn or South Africa's ability to control the market. These arguments ignore one factor: to date this has not been tested in the open market. No one is under any illusion that poaching of live rhino will cease should a legal trade be possible. Since the publication of *Rhino Keepers* in 2012, we, as authors, have refrained from taking a position one way or the other, but five years have passed since that date and we have grave doubts about the upkeep of ongoing costs associated with the wellbeing of the species. We are not passive bystanders or onlookers – we are active participants and know only too well what it takes to sustain the battle. Outsiders must understand this is not just a battle for the soul of the rhino. The implications of criminal activity arising from the killing of a rhino are far-reaching.

Unfortunately, in the world today there are opposing forces with regard to the question of a legal trade in rhino horn. The pro-trade lobbyists are perceived as being wealthy landowners who see an opportunity to increase their wealth by the sale of

The value in dollar terms of a living rhino is enormous, as described by Profs Saayman and Saayman in Chapter 3. Photo: Wilderness Safaris/Dana Allen.

harvested rhino horn. To many out there it may well be seen as nothing more than getting into bed with criminals of the worst type. Trade, as such, has a bad name and the world is awash with examples of the illegal exploitation of wildlife species. The reaction of distaste and loathing is easy and understandable. The pro-trade lobbyists must recognise that, in their efforts to highlight the crisis by using graphic images of dead and dying rhino, a cynical perception may well exist.

The pro-trade lobbyists need to shift that focus as a matter of urgency. This is not about creating wealth for the privileged few who own rhino. It is far more important than that, as indicated in Chapter 3 by the two Saayman professors. The wider value of the living animal needs to be the main focus. Unfortunately, the move to push for a legal local trade has not helped either, with the wrong perception being created.

In order to support the principle of rhino horn trade, we believe that owners of rhino horn must contribute a percentage of earnings into a special fund that will manage the process and not be a burden on the state. The pro-trade organisations need to strengthen their ties with the DEA in finding solutions to this important issue. Finally, we need to recognise the existence of potential opponents of an international trade in rhino horn who may well perceive the lifting of any ban as a direct threat to their very being.

When considering the rhino trade debate, it's important to understand that the harvesting of rhino horn is an option for the trade. Harvesting of rhino horn does not require killing the animal to obtain it as is the case with an elephant's ivory. Rhino horn is made of keratin and is the same substance as finger nails and similar to compressed hair. The horn grows continually throughout the animal's life. If cut off, it regrows at the rate of about 10 cm per year, subject of course to normal wear through rubbing, which varies according to the animal's behaviour and environment (but care must be taken not to cut too close to the base, damaging nerves and blood vessels).

Rhino have developed horns as an important component in their feeding and defensive behaviour. However, dehorning has been carried out in captive and wild populations as a poaching deterrent.

If private rhino owners and government-run protected areas could legally sell harvested horn, they would be in a significantly different position than they are today.

To highlight the above suggestion, we urge readers to go to www.rhinoalive.com for a more detailed analysis.

CITES action and inaction

The Convention on International Trade in Endangered Species (CITES) ban on trade in rhino horn and body parts came into effect in 1976. Clearly, the ban has not prevented the slaughter of African rhinos. Given the massive upsurge in poaching since 2008, where is the evidence to prove that the campaigns to convince Southeast Asia to seek alternatives are succeeding? The whole issue of trade bans in the case of the rhino is most controversial and has been for some time.

Endeavours to have the ban overturned are not new in South Africa. An attempt took place as early as the 8th Conference of the Parties (CoP8) in Kyoto, Japan, in March 1992:

> The reasons behind the proposal were simple – after 15 years of total CITES protection, the world status of rhino populations, with the exception of the southern race of the white rhinoceros, had steadily worsened. The CITES ban (and within the country bans on trade) had apparently merely exacerbated a deteriorating situation with no indication of any change in trend. Both South Africa and Zimbabwe feel that a new approach to the conservation of rhinoceros is necessary.[20]

The proposal from South Africa at CoP10 in 1997 was to remove the restrictions placed on the southern African white rhino at CoP9. These restrictions prohibited trade in rhino horn and other products. South Africa had asked for a zero quota, meaning that no trade would be conducted until the next conference. This was done so that a set of controls could be put in place before actual trading resumed, and to allow South Africa to deal openly with the authorities of consumer countries without any potential negative political ramifications.

The South African proposal to legalise trade in rhino products was rejected by one vote on 18 June 1997, with 60 in favour and 32 against, but needing a two-thirds majority. The South African delegation made a strategic error by not insisting on a secret ballot the first time around. The CITES secretariat wanted to finish the issue the same day, since it was late, and South Africa accommodated them by agreeing to a public vote for both the elephant and rhino proposals. It thus came as a shock when, in the second vote on 19 June, by secret ballot, the proposal was rejected with 54 votes in favour and 48 against – far from the required two-thirds majority.[21]

CoP17 has come and gone, where the Swaziland proposal to trade in horn was defeated by 100 against, with 26 in favour and 17 abstentions. Not surprisingly, South Africa's DEA as host to this CoP spared itself, in our opinion, embarrassment by not submitting a proposal, knowing full well that it too would be defeated. We continue to wrangle over resolutions, and rhinos continue to die. Is there any reason for hope at CoP18?

In summing up CoP17, Eugene Lapointe, former secretary-general of CITES, had this to say:

Madam Chair, due to the important increase in poaching and in related illegal wildlife activities, the international community has reinstated the 'inquisition' in order to identify the witch or witches responsible for this drama. The inquisition quickly identified trade as the culprit and therefore the witch to be burnt.

However, we cannot burn trade; it is a concept – most likely the most important concept in the history of humankind – that has allowed societies, communities and peoples to link together. So we decided instead to burn the symbols of the concept, i.e. ivory tusks, rhino horns and other confiscated wildlife specimens. But while the bonfire was on, we threw in it the history book that tells us that prohibitions do not work, have never worked and never will work.

On the same occasion, we threw in the bonfire the dictionary of definitions to replace it by our own. As such, the definition of a hunter and a poacher are the same. There is no different definition between legal trade and illegal trade: harvesting a wild animal is called murder; a skilled ivory carver is considered a forger; bribery to a poor game warden is corruption; bribery to a senior official or politician is commitment to environment; and so on.

All these new definitions mixing legalities with illegalities together then fall under the general definition of 'wildlife crime', a message that celebrities, crowned or not, are happy to carry throughout the world.

Finally Madam Chair, we threw in the bonfire, the Charter of Human Rights and quickly replaced it by the Charter of Animal Rights and the Poachers' Charter. And this with dramatic consequences for people.[22]

We should not be so naïve as to think a legal trade in rhino horn will halt poaching. It will not. Trade in diamonds and gold in South Africa is illegal, but smuggling of both continues in spite of legislation. G. Swanepoel said, 'Legalisation without any proper counter measures such as strict controls will only create a parallel opportunity for the illegal trade to exist with the legal.'[23]

Every minute, every hour, every day China changes, so the saying goes. We may not need to despair forever as the China today is not the China of old, and its modernisation may eventually yield public opinion that is as appalled by the destruction of wildlife species as we are.

But if there is to be any action from China or other Asian countries that benefits the rhino, we have not yet seen the remotest hint of it.

So, which way the rhino?

In 1859 in *The Origin of Species*, Charles Darwin wrote: 'A fair result can be obtained only by fully stating and balancing the facts and arguments on both sides of each question'. Surely it is not too late for us to heed his words. In 2012 Dr Michael Knight, now chair of the AfRSG, and Dr Richard Emslie, its scientific officer, were of a similar opinion regarding rhino conservation: 'We need an objective and rational look at the pros and cons of all alternative options to see which one or what combination of them was most likely succeed.'[24]

They listed some possibilities:

- Reduce illegal killing of rhinos (their number-one concern). *Little evidence to indicate this has happened; instead, the killing has soared.*
- Reduce black-market prices for horn in Southeast Asia. *In reality, the price has vastly increased.*
- Reduce market demand for illegal horn in Southeast Asia. *Not likely; there is nothing to indicate any change whatsoever.*
- Generate sufficient incentives to encourage the spread and continuation of rhinos onto private and community land (critical to expand range and keep numbers growing rapidly and to prevent overstocking and declines in performance in established populations). *This has to be very carefully considered given the current, ongoing rampant poaching.*
- Generate more and sustainable funding to increase law enforcement and intelligence to try to ensure we get to more poachers before they kill. *We believe this objective is indeed critical but not likely unless the funding could be guaranteed.*

Dr John Hanks, a highly respected conservationist, notes:

> The fact is that all the major NGOs and the AfRSG are silent on the main issue
> of concern, namely the total absence of sustainability of the majority of rhino
> conservation proposals, where there is no hope of maintaining the present level
> of funding by soliciting funding from donors every year. The only realistic way
> forward is for the international agencies and the few NGOs that still have any
> credibility to come together to make a serious appeal through the UN agencies
> for a renewed commitment to ensure that carefully selected designated
> protected areas receive the budgets they need to do their job properly.
>
> These areas are or should be the crown jewels for biodiversity conservation, and
> those areas that have no hope of being saved should be allowed to disappear.
> When coupled with the private sector and well-managed communal lands being
> allowed to generate income from consumptive use, we have some hope.[25]

The Kruger National Park is without doubt the most important jewel in South Africa's
crown, but its rhino are under serious threat, and protecting them is massively costly.
According to the economist Michael Eustace:

> The Kruger Park is 20 000 km² in extent and has a 400-km border with
> Mozambique. It would be prohibitively costly to patrol effectively. Kruger
> currently has 400 rangers who patrol the park, i.e. 50 km² per ranger. I doubt
> that one ranger could effectively protect more than 10 km² per day. This implies
> a force of 2 000 rangers or five times the current force. Assuming only half the
> park needs to be patrolled intensively, because rhino are concentrated in one
> half, then 1 000 rangers would be needed. The cost, including overheads, of an
> additional 600 rangers would approximate $10 million (R80 million) per year, or
> more than the annual surplus of SANParks, which was R52.6 million for the year
> to March 2011. It is not possible for SANParks to finance 1 000 rangers, and even
> if it were, there would still be a weakness that undermines law enforcement
> efforts in most parks in Africa: corruption among the law enforcers.[26]

The Kruger National Park is divided into 22 sections, each with a section ranger in charge.
In addition, there are specially trained anti-poaching operational units. How many are
fully operational at the highest level is not known, as this information is confidential,
like much other information where rhino are under intensive security. Is it adequate
and sustainable over time? Or is there a security budget shortfall like the R7 million
shortage faced by Ezemvelo KZN Wildlife?[27] Not surprisingly, as we saw in Chapter 2,
KwaZulu-Natal lost eight rhino in a week in their premier park and most important

stronghold in September 2016, on the eve of the CoP17 meeting in Johannesburg.

We strongly urge readers to refer to Dr John Hanks's much acclaimed book, *Operation Lock and the War on Rhino Poaching*, which provides more information on the threat facing rhinos and the enormous costs of protecting this species. We recommend also reading a key reference on the subject of the IUCN's sustainable financing of protected areas: a global review.[28]

There is a body of opinion that believes that if private owners turn their backs on the rhino because of the risks and dangers associated with keeping them, the value of living rhino will plummet, and there are signs of this beginning to appear. If that happens, then those who rely on sale of live rhino – such as the SANParks, Ezemvelo KZN Wildlife and private owners with surplus animals who plough that money back into conservation – may well be facing a very different scenario.

Perhaps what we need to realise is that no matter what the trade ban outcome is in the years to come, or whether a legal trade can make a difference, or whether ranchers abandon the rhino, we are always going to have private sanctuaries and government reserves, where the bottom line is not about the rhino's contribution to the balance sheet. Poaching will probably always occur. Rhino are not immortal – they die, just like everything else.

We also need to reconsider the strategy of rhino population expansion as a principal objective, and focus instead on having fewer rhino in the long run, and in fewer sanctuaries, and only in areas where they can be properly protected. We should also ponder whether we inadvertently contributed to the current disastrous wave of poaching by being overly committed to trying to expand rhino populations. The original impulse for this back in 1994 was fear that we were in danger of seeing the species disappear – we wanted more rhinos in more reserves. Indeed black rhino numbers did climb, much to the satisfaction of all involved. But then in 2008 things changed. At first the main victim, the Kruger National Park, appeared unconcerned, but they are certainly not any longer.

That one of the world's most magnificent creatures is reduced once again to endless argument is an indictment of our best ideas so far. We now need better ideas. What will history say of us if we allow the slaughter to continue and extinction to happen because we could not work out how to prevail over the criminal syndicates of Asia? One thing we are all certain of is that the rhino will not survive without our help, and every single option available to us should be considered.

We have to demonstrate to the world that we can dig ourselves out of this black hole and restore the rhino to dignity and security once and for all. It won't be the first time we've done it.

What we need is a 'Rhino Revolution'.

CHAPTER 5

Monitoring black rhino

A CASE STUDY OF BLACK RHINO IN NATIONAL PARKS, 2002–2016

By Lucky Mavrandonis and Sue Downie

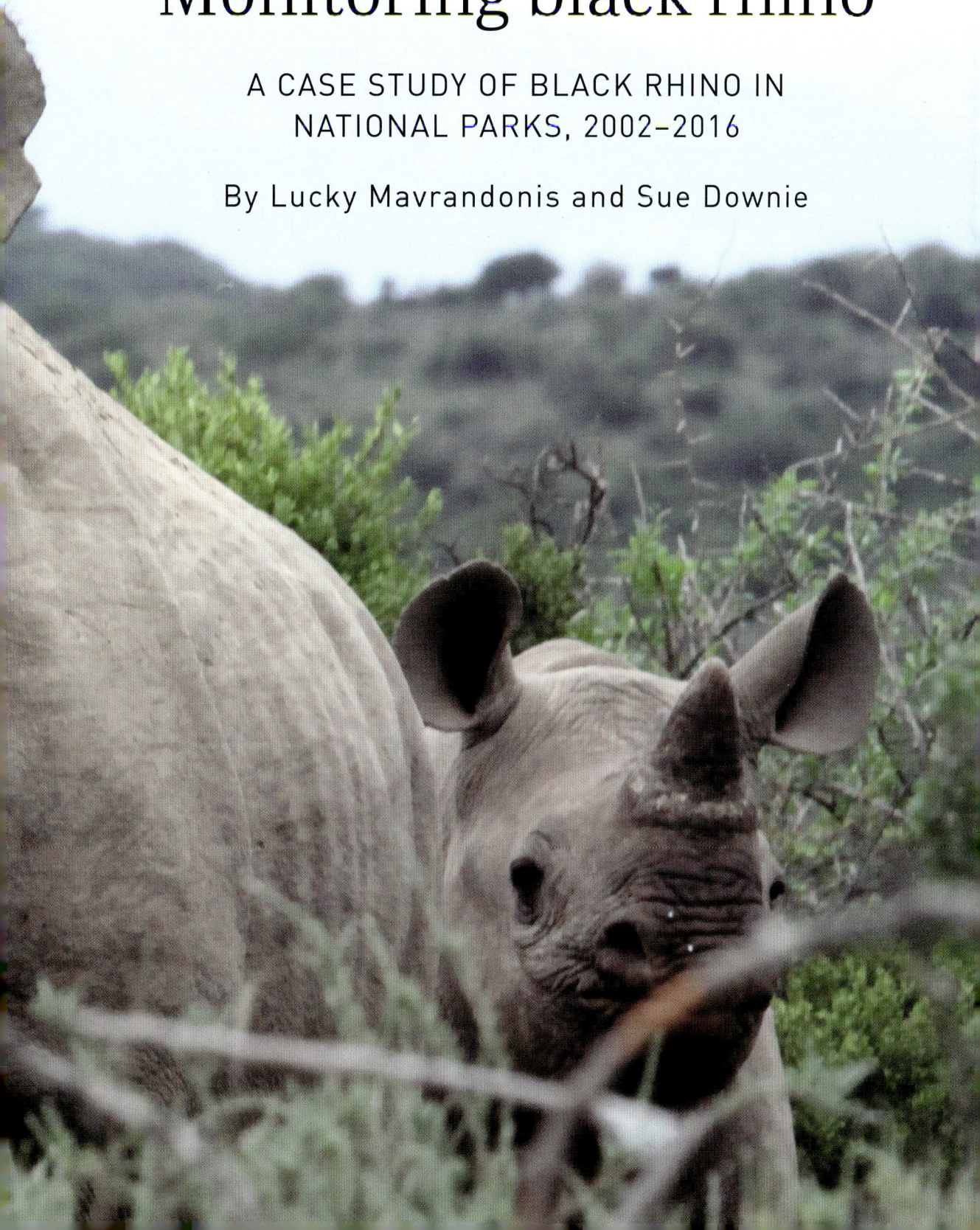

*It is now more than 20 years since Sue and Lucky began to work on the conservation of the black rhinoceros in South Africa ... These efforts have made large new areas of habitat available for the southwest arid zone subspecies of the black rhinoceros, **Diceros bicornis bicornis**. On their watch a handful of these animals have grown into thriving populations ... The monitoring of reintroduced black rhinoceros populations by Sue and Lucky has produced an impressive body of biological information of great value to science and to practical conservation.*[1]

– Dr Anthony Hall-Martin, 18 February 2012

How the case study of monitoring began

Anthony Hall-Martin, a man of true vision, was far ahead of his time. His vision fuelled our passion and fund-raising abilities for our study on the black rhino subspecies (*Diceros bicornis bicornis*), and this resulted in generous sponsorships from the David Shepherd Wildlife Foundation (DSWF), Sasol, WildAid and others in order to expand two national parks, not only for the benefit of black rhino, but also more importantly to increase the habitat.

Our dedication to black rhinos was inspired in 1991 by a very special rhino, Shibula. At Anthony's request, funds raised were used to return Shibula to southern Africa from Lisbon Zoo in Portugal. After two years in a concrete enclosure, Shibula was back in Africa. By May 2012, she had given birth to eight calves – an all-too-rare, good news, conservation story.

After sporadically visiting Shibula from 1991 to 2001, and seeing her first two calves very close up, our lives changed forever. Our passion and dedication to black rhinos goes way beyond a short-term, self-serving, research project.

In January 2002 we applied to DSWF to fund a year of monitoring the black rhino. Incredibly, they covered the major portion for 10 years at a cost of R3.46 million (£266 000). The project study areas were four smaller national parks, and for security reasons, we prefer to use letters of the Greek alphabet to refer to them: Alpha, Beta, Gamma and Delta. The total study area was 1 825 km².

The necessity for accurately monitoring black rhino populations is not debateable – it is essential for such a valuable endangered species, especially during the current poaching crisis. Monitoring involves locating, identifying and observing rhinos by using a combination of methods and techniques, including telemetry, tracking spoor and searching from vantage points with a spotting scope to identify individuals by means of unique ear-notches.

With regular dedicated and focused monitoring, we have data on each and every black rhino in the four populations. We started with a handful of individuals and were caring for 14-fold the original number at the end (specific numbers withheld as a security precaution). We collected data over 14 years in the field, which was accurate, reliable and consistent, and provided meaningful information for analysis. We personally collected all field data.

OPPOSITE: Shibula's first morning back in southern Africa, August 1991. Photo: Lucky Mavrandonis.

PREVIOUS SPREAD: Sasha with her male calf Vukile who is 10 months old. 18 April 2012. Photo: Lucky Mavrandonis.

Our goals were:

- to positively identify at least 75% of rhinos on each trip (we achieved 77.7%);
- very importantly, to ensure we remained undetected by rhinos in 80% of sightings (achieved 82.5%);
- to attempt to see 100% of all rhinos each year (achieved 97%);
- to assess the body-condition of all rhinos identified;
- to record all details of each sighting immediately;
- to be in the veld at our planned position at least 30 minutes before sunrise until at least 30 minutes after sunset; and
- to always respect the rhinos and ensure their safety – if the wind changed, we would abandon the sighting.

Successful monitoring was a huge learning curve. We were totally ignorant, and not much was expected of us – only to find spoor and dung. We sought help from passionate rhino people such as Blythe Loutit in Namibia (we were shown how they tracked desert rhino) and Clive Walker in the Waterberg, together with David Bradfield and his rangers.

STATISTICS (2002–2012)

Number of field trips	150
Trip days including travel	1 406
Days in the field	1 150
Black rhinos in sight (in hours)	1 416
% population identified per trip	77.7%
% sightings with rhinos undisturbed	82.5%
Total number of digital photographs	89 968
Video footage (in hours)	105
Tracked on foot in km (last 5½ years)	1 243
Average per trip on foot in km (last 5½ years)	27.8
Maximum km on foot in one trip	73
Km travelled in study areas (last 5½ years)	35 586
Total km, including travel (last 5½ years)	149 933
Estimated km in 14 years	374 000
Black rhino sightings (5½ years)	620

STATISTICS (2002–2012)

Maximum hours with rhinos in sight on a trip	24.5
Average working day (in hours)	13
% sightings with more than one group (a group denotes one single rhino or a cow with calf)	26.5%

We made every effort to be unobtrusive. As a result we observed natural black rhino behaviour, interactions and a few matings. However, we had several unexpected, adrenalin-producing close encounters, but never hurt or were injured by any of the animals – rhinos, buffalo or lions. And we never carried a gun.

Our major technique was to find rhinos from high-vantage points, identify them with the scope, and then assess how to get closer without being detected. We could often get to within 50 metres, and then stayed as long as possible observing and photographing. Our 'scientific' objectives evolved:

• to assess the population performance;
• to facilitate the development of appropriate management strategies; and
• to assess the dispersal into new habitats after relocation.

Faru and Petra (two-and-a-half-month-old female calf), 15 May 2009. Photo: Lucky Mavrandonis.

Khora and Nomvula (a 10-day-old female calf), 19 February 2005. We waited five hours to identify the mother, as it was her first calf and she was the first tiny wild calf we found. Photo: Lucky Mavrandonis.

We also funded and assisted in the implementation of park-specific security plans.

Patience and passion for knowledge of this magnificent ancient herbivore made every day an adventure filled with excitement.

From vantage points with the wind in our favour, we have observed rhinos greeting, calves playing, groups of five, six, up to 11 rhino socialising, bulls sparring, cows chasing off calves to give birth again, a cow and bull mating nine times, a cow and bull mating with a calf browsing calmly close by, a three-month-old calf greeting her father – these are just a few of the many interactions observed in these actively social rhinos. Observations have been as close as 25 metres without the rhinos being aware of our presence.

We often worked separately to double the coverage. This increased the danger significantly as it meant hiking alone with the ever-present possibility of bumping into rhinos, buffaloes or lions – which did happen!

With the wind in our favour we have walked 30 to 40 metres behind rhinos – a very intense privilege. At times of unexpected close contact in thick bush, once they had assessed the threat, they turned and ran away.

High-quality equipment is essential: binoculars, 20–60x spotting scope, range finder, camera, 100–400 lens, video, maps, GPS, transmitters, camera traps and up-to-date ear-notch charts for positive identification. Regular use of the telemetry paid dividends in being able to triangulate and pinpoint a position.

TOP: Six black rhino browsing together, 10 February 2010. They browsed and interacted for three and a half hours. Photo: Lucky Mavrandonis.

BOTTOM: Ombika (father) and Vuya (a three-month-old female calf), 29 May 2009. Ombika and the other bull, Alfred, had been sparring within 50 metres of Dundi and her first calf Vuya, when she walked out to greet the bulls. Little Vuya also greeted her father with proper rhino etiquette. Photo: Lucky Mavrandonis.

On every trip we added to the population information and developed family trees with historic data from Anthony and Dr Guy Castley. Soon we could accurately forecast births and query unexpected assumptions by field rangers. The precise data allowed for informed analysis, followed by recommendations to national parks, regarding over population, adverse sex ratios and slowing population growth. Some recommendations were implemented and sadly some suggestions were ignored. Being independent was a major factor in ensuring accurate information, as we were never in a position of having to produce results for monthly reports.

Within a week after every trip, a detailed report with photographs was sent to the section ranger and park manager as well as other interested people.

In summary, we completed 150 trips in 14 years, roughly 11 per year, each lasting 10 to 12 days. We also did a number of intensive monitoring trips of up to 42 consecutive days. We observed rhinos for 1 416 hours!

After following Sukulu's transmitter signal, we found her in a dry riverbed. Photo: Lucky Mavrandonis.

Relocations and rehabilitations

In the mid-1980s, because all the south-western subspecies in South Africa had been killed, national parks started new populations by translocating a small number from Namibia. In 1989 South Africa had less than 20 black rhino of this subspecies. Our project alone has helped quadruple that number.

Both relocations and rehabilitations were used to manage the population in the study period. Although we monitored four separate small populations, the rhinos were all the same subspecies, therefore they were managed as one meta-population. Rhinos were relocated as required to improve their breeding success. We observed many introductions and relocations and recorded the results. After a few years we carefully analysed the population dynamics in the four areas and the results were clear. We submitted a report with suggestions and recommendations to national parks.

POPULATION CONSTRAINTS & RECOMMENDATIONS

Area	Problems	Interventions
Alpha	None	None
Beta	Carrying capacity exceeded; too many females	Remove sub-adult females
Gamma	Carrying capacity exceeded; too many male calves	Remove sub-adult males to another reserve
Delta	Too few rhinos; too few breeding females	Introduce sub-adult females from Beta

Relocations have inherent risks and should not be undertaken lightly. However, with the goal of improving the meta-population's growth rate and genetic pool, the relocations were approved and took place in May 2012 and May 2013.

Because there are so few black rhino of this subspecies, our project also proved the usefulness of rehabilitation and introduction into a wild population. As mentioned earlier, Shibula was returned to Africa after two years in a zoo, and had become very tame. It was Anthony's idea to return her to the wild in South Africa, as she was the only black rhino of her subspecies in Europe with very little chance of breeding. It was very well thought out, and it was a long, slow and ultimately very successful process.

Shibula became a celebrity with her journey covered by the TV programme 50/50. The SA Air Force flew her on a C130 from Cape Town and the army transported her crate to the boma. Her 13-day return to Africa involved 8 560 km by sea, 820 km by air and 127 km by road. After several months in the boma, being weaned off the zoo diet, acclimatising to the local natural browse, and safely meeting the resident rhino, it was time to fend for herself.

When the gate of her boma was opened before sunrise on a clear summer morning, she took her time slowly assessing what was happening. A few of us were sitting on top of her transport crate. Before she walked off into the veld, she came

Shibula and Dundi in 1995. Shibula, still accustomed to humans, brought her calf up close to meet us. Photo: Lucky Mavrandonis.

TOP: Thandi and Mia with Sue Downie, 23 November 2008. Photo: Lucky Mavrandonis.

BOTTOM: Thandi and Mia 'swimming', 27 November 2008. Photo: Sue Downie.

back, lifted her head to smell Anthony's hand – as if to thank him for her freedom, an unexpected empathy between pachyderm and human.

The results were phenomenal – by May 2012 Shibula had given birth to eight calves with a ninth due at year end. Two of her daughters had five calves between them. Rehabilitation into the wild had resulted in 14 more black rhinos in 18 years.

In another rehabilitation, Thandi arrived unexpectedly. Her mother Sasha had given birth in a holding boma after relocation from Namibia. Baby Thandi was separated during the night and was found cold and alone at first light. Concerned that Sasha may reject Thandi, she was airlifted by helicopter to a rehabilitation centre.

We visited Thandi every month to photograph and monitor her progress – a unique opportunity to study this rare and endangered mammal at such close quarters. When she was nine months old, we assisted in her move back to her birthplace as she had chronic diarrhoea and needed to ingest natural browse. When she was two, she was moved into a fenced enclosure of 400 hectares to begin breaking the human contact. She was then joined by a very young, wild-born female called Mia and they formed a close bond. When Thandi was 5½ years old, she and Mia were relocated to a very large arid park, and we monitored their introduction intensively until we were sure they could find water and adapt to the new browse, as well as meet the resident rhinos.

After brief stays in a boma, then a fenced release camp, the gate was opened late one afternoon. This was a critical time for them as two years earlier a young female had died after a veld-to-veld introduction. Thandi had only known a concrete reservoir from which to drink water and Mia was only three years old.

On the third morning they were on top of a high hill with a very steep slope. It was getting hot on the treeless koppie and not a cloud in the sky. We established that they had not found any water since the previous morning. They must have been thirsty, and did not know where to find any and could not find their way down – a very stressful situation.

The field rangers knew an easier way down. We had 20-litre containers of water and two troughs. We believed that intervention to assist the rhinos was essential. After all what was the point of all the effort by so many people if we left them to die like the other young rhino? It was 38°C at midday and they had no shade or water. We carried 60 litres of water and the troughs up the hill. Both drank thirstily and then Thandi followed us, as did Mia, squeaking constantly, as they walked down with Sue … incredible trust and communication. It rained soon after that and we found them 'swimming' in an old farm dam.

Both rhino have adapted, and had one calf each by May 2012. Another successful rehabilitation, and a good boost to the rhino numbers.

Astounding results

Thandi, heavily pregnant, 19 September 2010. Photo: Lucky Mavrandonis.

Regular unobtrusive monitoring over 14 years gave us spectacularly accurate results in this case study, because in over 80% of observations, rhinos were not aware of us watching them. We were able to accurately record the details of every calf: the date of birth, who the father was and establish its sex quite soon – all the essential information to create family trees.

In our published paper,[2] the growth rate for the four populations was calculated as +13.4% per year, which is much higher than the estimated average of 5% in the literature for black rhinos. This growth of 13.4% is even more impressive as it included many negative influences, from different introduction dates in each park, to very small founder populations, as well as introduction of sexually immature rhinos. Also included was one incident of a newly introduced bull causing the death of six rhinos, including three females in 2005 and 2006. This single incident resulted in the death of 31.6% of this park's population.

A better gauge of real growth is the last six years (2007–2012), which eliminated most negative influences. An incredible growth of 16.5% per year, which was consistent whether calculating for the last five, four or three years. This underscores the potential of a safe and undisturbed population.

Meta-population % growth rates over different periods

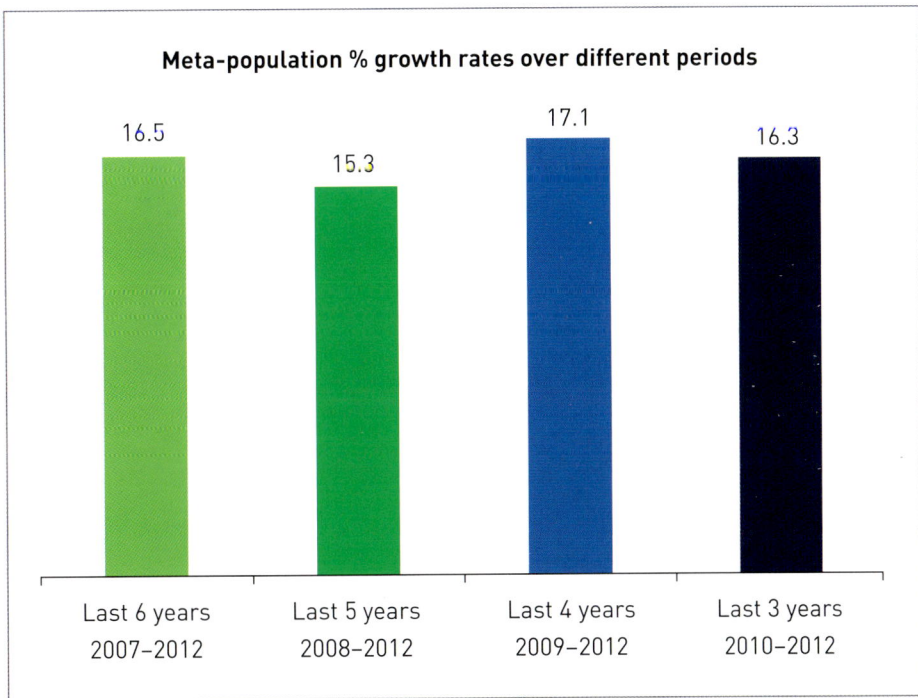

16.5	15.3	17.1	16.3
Last 6 years 2007–2012	Last 5 years 2008–2012	Last 4 years 2009–2012	Last 3 years 2010–2012

There are several factors that contributed to this successful breeding population, especially when starting with only a few rhino. Obviously good habitat is one of the factors that is essential in keeping their body condition good.

As the population increased, there were six reproductive indicators[3] that we measured. The four project areas together were rated good to excellent in five of these, and only one indicator was rated as moderate to good.

We recorded 65 births, including Shibula's first two calves. We calculated an accurate gestation for one female of between 15.3 and 15.58 months. We observed three matings – one from a distance of 102 metres when the bull mounted the cow nine times in four hours. During another mating, a 19-month-old calf browsed close to the couple and was never threatened or chased away.

Over the 10-year-period, the mortality rate was 2.6%, which is lower than the accepted level of 3–4%. However, natural deaths only accounted for 18%, while human-induced deaths were responsible for 82% (poor management decisions, human disturbance and relocations).

Dhora (female) and Kaba (male), 10 April 2008. Photo: Lucky Mavrandonis.

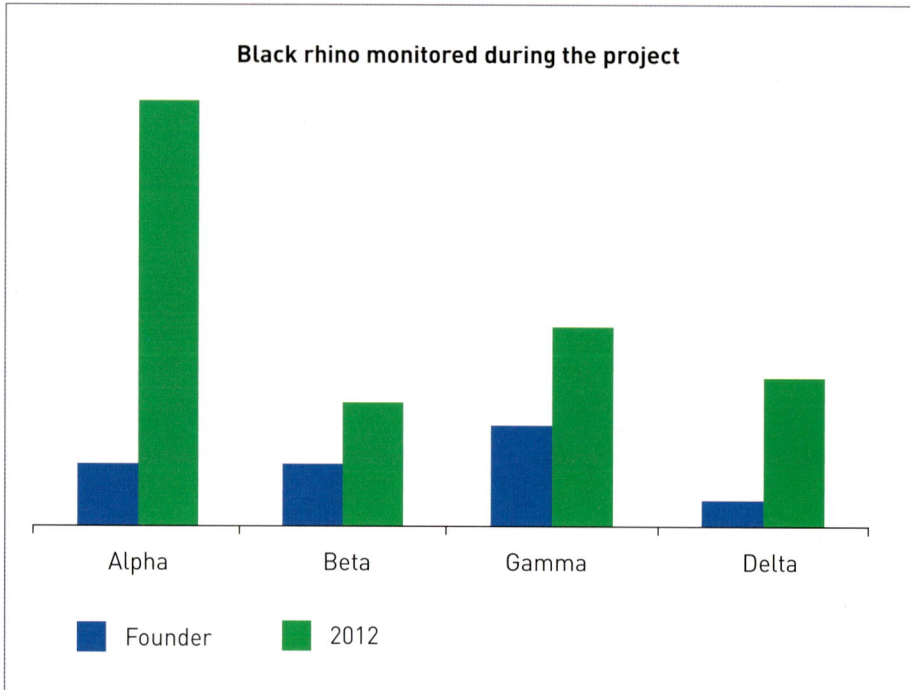

Black rhino monitored during the project

If we include the years 2013–2016 in only one park, the mortality increased due to a poor management decision. National parks, after doing a 'risk analysis', introduced the same bull responsible for the six deaths in 2005/2006. We opposed this decision because of his aggressive history, and the availability of other unrelated males. This time three rhinos died in 2013 and 2014. The logical assumption was that the same bull was responsible.

Our project started in 2002 with only a handful of rhinos in one park, and in May 2012 the total population in all four parks had increased 14-fold. We know the numbers are small, growth can be over-simplified and deceptive in small populations, but the study is on a subspecies where the numbers are inherently very small. In 2012 our project accounted for 56% of national parks or a third of South Africa's total population of this subspecies of black rhino, therefore the numbers are significant. Even if we include Namibia's population, the world has less than 2500 of this subspecies.

Our results are real, based on visual observations and positive identification of known individuals. No manipulated scientific models or assumptions were needed.

There are some myths about black rhino that we disproved in the populations we studied. Scientists call black rhinos 'solitary' because they do not live in herds. It may be that in arid areas food is not abundant and they are found browsing far apart. But we observed up to 11 rhinos socialising for several hours at a time. They have a 'greeting' ritual and know each individual in their population. In 26.5% of our observations we observed more than one group together, i.e. a group denoted as a single rhino or a cow with calf.

Bulls did not attack calves when mating with the mother. Competition between bulls is not necessary for successful breeding – a better breeding rate is achieved if the bull concentrates on courting the females and making 'babies', rather than fighting with other bulls.

Black rhinos' eyesight is not as poor as 'they say'. Rhinos have fair, if narrow, binocular vision, and they often turn their head from side to side to get a better view. They do, however, have excellent motion detection, which, together with superb hearing and smell, allows them to pinpoint an intruder (human or other) incredibly quickly. Snorting elicits movement!

We have never found black rhinos to be aggressive, even though we have on many occasions unexpectedly 'bumped' into them. They are inquisitive and want to assess the threat, but usually in our experience they run or walk away. They are big, incredibly nimble and quick, so if a calf is scared or threatened, or an exit blocked, they would charge the threat, and it could be very dangerous.

Effective monitoring – an expensive and long-term undertaking

The black rhino is difficult to monitor due to its preferred habitat. They are mainly nocturnal, with the best sightings usually occuring early morning and late afternoon.

It cost national parks nothing for our black rhino monitoring project. Besides the fund-raising and donations, the project sponsored transmitters, helicopter flying time and security, among other things. National parks received all pertinent information verbally after every monitoring trip, as well as a written report within a week.

Only our direct costs were sponsored during our project, such as airfares, diesel, accommodation and equipment. We volunteered our services and time for 14 years. There were two direct sponsors: DSWF and ourselves personally, while national parks contributed 'in-kind'.

BREAKDOWN OF COSTS AND SPONSORSHIP

DSWF	R3 460 000	69%
Ourselves personally	R1 470 000	30%
National parks	R 73 000	1%
	R5 003 000	100%

National parks' contribution allowed us to stay in tourist accommodation at no charge, mainly in one park, if the camp was not fully booked. In another park we paid the full price, but could occasionally take advantage of a pensioner's discount!

The R5 million covered all monitoring costs for 14 years, including security from late 2010, plus a special donation of R185 000 for transport of rhinos from Namibia. Monitoring itself cost R3.04 million with security amounting to R1.7 million.

R5 million may sound a lot, but to protect all our project's highly endangered rhinos over 14 years, it is a valuable investment. In the last three years, we have been monitoring in one park only, at a cost of R7 475 per rhino per year. In the four areas during our monitoring, no rhinos were lost to poaching.

This 14-year study by external researchers with international and local funding has proven that the four sub-populations of this black rhino subspecies – given good habitat and limited human interference – can breed at a rate of 13% per year over 14 years, and will contribute significantly to the survival of the subspecies by exceeding South Africa's Biodiversity Management Plan targets and growth rate of 5%.

However, is there the will to make the effort required to make more land available, improve the levels of monitoring and do what is best for the rhinos?

Factors essential to continuing this success are:

- Careful and unobtrusive monitoring to ensure reproductive indicators remain positive. Relocations should be undertaken only when necessary.
- Black rhinos breed best when there is minimum tourist impact. Areas should be dedicated for breeding with limited tourist access, with one or two areas specifically for 'surplus' bulls where tourists can see black rhinos.
- Beta is an example of how high-tourist density and intrusive monitoring impacted negatively on the animals. One month after the abrupt termination of the project, a field ranger was severely injured by a cow that had been separated from her calf. The calf later died. Beta should not be a breeding area, but rather a camp for 'surplus' bulls that would satisfy tourists.
- Long-term investment and partnership with the private sector can play a pivotal role in developing rhino areas, as well as monitoring them to provide independent analysis of progress and performance.
- Our birth forecast indicates it is imperative to acquire new areas of suitable habitat for black rhino. This is the single most important component to ensure the future of the species.
- The study also validates the value of a long-term investment to rehabilitate rhinos. In this study, two rehabilitated females resulted in 18 additional rhinos.
- Formal ethology (behaviour) studies should be pursued to better understand black rhinos, but observations should be unobtrusive – which our study proved is possible.
- Above all, a dedicated senior rhino manager or coordinator is vital for the future of rhinos in national parks.
- Respect for dedicated external researchers working closely and sharing information with national parks is essential.

We do not believe that a parastatal has the staff or funds to dedicate to proper black rhino monitoring and security. Also, independent input is vital to keep information accurate and relevant. External researchers should be encouraged.

Researchers should have the passion to dedicate time and financial resources for a long-term study. They should be totally independent and always put the rhinos first. Meticulous fieldwork is essential for meaningful results and analysis. Computer models/assumptions do not give accurate results.

Some disparage the field study of small populations, but sadly the reality is that there are very few black rhinos left – so it is all we have. Respect is also overdue locally for a conservation attitude to research. This was acknowledged by the 2013 symposium[4] in the session dealing with Population Dynamics and Conservation.

Simplistically, more passion means more knowledge,
better management and improved growth.

Termination of the project

In May 2012 the project was terminated in three of four areas after 10 years of regular monthly monitoring – in fact our 25-year involvement went back to 1991.

The termination by the regional manager in charge of the three parks was abrupt. The dispute involved computer access codes for GPS satellite foot collars sponsored by ourselves. Transmitter frequencies were always given to the section ranger who was directly responsible for the rhinos, and he was also given the access codes. But with new GPS technology, there were huge security risks, and we were not prepared to compromise security ethics by letting anyone else have the codes. Namibian authorities were much stricter.

Senior directors and the chairman of the African Rhino Specialist Group (AfRSG) met with us in an attempt to reconcile the disparate views, but the regional manager refused to meet us. However, we were asked to continue in the remaining park and did so up to January 2016, when we received an email from an employee to the effect that it 'had come to their attention' that our 'research agreement' had come to an end and we were 'not permitted to conduct any further fieldwork in the park for the project'. In fact the research agreement was with Dr Anthony Hall-Martin, who had sadly died in May 2014.

We do understand that rules are rules, but are they so disinterested and short-sighted not to realise that this is not just a research project, and that we provided an essential service to park management on the black rhinos in their parks?

Our gratitude goes to Anthony Hall-Martin for his support and help, always given freely – his death was a huge loss to rhinos and to many of us personally. We are grateful to David and Melanie Shepherd who tirelessly raised funds for the project. Dr Hector Magome also gave us enthusiastic support and encouragement. The field rangers and the Bushman (San) we worked with in the veld showed great interest in learning about our unobtrusive method of monitoring rhinos, and we found their work ethic amazing. The biggest compliment we were paid by the rangers was that we made them feel that they were important.

We have enormous respect for these magnificent animals, their majesty, competence and power. To see them run with their smooth, elegant, fluid and efficient style, reaching a top speed of over 40 km/h in a matter of 2.5 seconds, is one of the most awesome things to watch. Our years of walking with black rhinos has been an exceptional experience and a privilege.

FOLLOWING PAGE: Protect the elephant and you protect whole ecosystems. The African elephant is currently diminishing across much of Africa, whereas in southern Africa the opposite is the case. However, we need to guard against complacency. Photo: Wilderness Safaris/Dana Allen.

CHAPTER 6

Black rhino, white rhino – what's in a name?

THE STORIES AND STUDIES BEHIND THE NAMES

By Jim Feely[1]

If all beasts were gone, man would die from a great loneliness of spirit. For whatever happens to the beasts, soon happens to man. All things are connected.

– Chief Seattle, Suquamish tribe and Duwamish chief, 1854

Dispelling the myth

It has been fascinating in my lifetime to witness the birth, growth and acceptance of a piece of pseudohistory and the legend that it is comprised of. This chapter is the widely accepted explanation of how the white rhino (Ceratotherium simum) got its name, which is such an inaccurate description of its outward appearance. Its skin colour is largely determined by the soil of its surroundings, overlaid on a medium-grey colour by its wallowing in mud and rolling in dust, as it is too for the black rhino (Diceros bicornis).

In the 18th and 19th centuries Afrikaner hunters called the white rhino the wijd (mond) renoster (wide [mouth] rhinoceros) in colloquial Dutch and Afrikaans. When early English-speaking travellers and hunters heard this name, they mistook the sound of wijd (weid, weit, wyd) for 'white', hence the English name.

The earliest mention in English of the name white rhino was made by John Barrow[2] in describing his travels in Namaqualand in the present Northern Cape during 1798. There he met a Griqua Afrikaner who told him that in his youth he had killed 'seven camelopardales [giraffes] and three white rhinoceroses in one day'[3] but did not say where. This conversation must have been conducted in Dutch or Afrikaans, the informant using kameelperde and wit(te)renosters, and not their English translations.

The earliest written use in Dutch of both the names, white and black rhino, was made by Petrus Borcherds in a letter to his father in 1802.[4] Borcherds, then in his teens, acted as assistant secretary and scribe to the commissioners of the Truter-Somerville expedition to the Tswana people at Dithakong (earlier known as Lattakoe), north-east of Kuruman in 1801–1802. Their report to the Cape governor was submitted in English,[5] but Borcherds had probably prepared the original draft in Dutch. (Where some minor discrepancies occur between these accounts, such as in dates/spelling, I have followed the official report.) His first observation referred to a male of the 'black variety' of rhino killed by Jacobus Kruger near Kuruman on 27 December 1801.[6] The second described a female 'white' rhino killed south of Kuruman by Kruger and Meintjes van den Bergh on 30 December 1801. In a separate account written in English by William Somerville, the first animal killed was called a 'black two-horned rhinoceros' with no mention being made of the second animal.

OPPOSITE: The notches in both ears of this black rhino enable 'monitors' to identify the animal in the field and to record details of condition and position. Photo: Dana Allen.

PREVIOUS SPREAD: An unusual picture of both a black rhino and a white rhino at a waterhole. Photo: Clive Walker.

Of the first rhino killed, it was noted that the 'upper lip was more pointed and hung over the lower lip' as Somerville also recorded. The Setswana name was seikloa, the name (keitloa) for the black rhino used during the 19th century. It was recorded that the upper lip of the second animal killed was 'more flat', and that its Setswana name was magooe, which is clearly a phonetic rendering of the name mogohu still recently in use for the white rhino.

These accounts confirm conclusively to me that the animal killed on 27 December 1801 was *D. bicornis*, and the one killed on 30 December was *C. simum*. The second animal was described as being smaller than the first, thereby indicating that it must have been immature, since an adult white rhino of either sex is larger than an adult black rhino.

Concerning the female rhino killed, Borcherds stated (in translation, original in Dutch): 'She was of the type known to us as the white rhinoceros ... I expected this animal to be entirely white according to its name, but found that she was a paler ash-grey than the black. I suppose that when the rain falls this animal is cleansed of mud and other impurities and will appear lighter at a distance, and put the derivation of the name down to that ....' Thus the oldest written record in Dutch is unequivocally of both 'black' and 'white' species under those names and not any other. Furthermore, the recorder himself saw and described the carcasses of both animals and gave their Setswana names in a way that identifies them beyond doubt, in my opinion. Clearly, the factoids are not true. Unfortunately, neither Borcherds, Truter nor Somerville asked Kruger how the names were derived.

Later in 1841, William Cornwallis Harris, an Indian army officer who was a visiting hunter and an accomplished artist, gave the names the 'square-nosed or white rhinoceros'. In the caption he gave witte rhinoster as the Cape colonists' name, and mohoohoo as the Setswana name. The latter is clearly another phonetic spelling of the modern name mogohu for the white rhino. In the caption that depicts the 'African rhinoceros' (black rhino, *D. bicornis*), Cornwallis Harris gave the colonists' name as rhinoster and the Setswana as borili.[7] He had hunted in both the present North West and Limpopo provinces in 1836.

A. Steedman recorded each species under the names black and white near Mafeking in 1826. Andrew Geddes Bain also noted 'white' rhino in the Mafeking area in 1826, and both rhinos under these names on a tributary of the Molopo River in 1834, while James Alexander (1838) likewise recorded both species with these names in central Namibia in 1836/37.

Thereafter, throughout the 19th century other hunters travelling in the white rhino's historical range and writing in English, such as Charles Andersson (1861), Thomas Baines (1864), William Baldwin (1894), Gordon Cumming (1850) and Fredrick Courtney Selous (1881, 1908), consistently used the names black rhino

TOP AND BOTTOM: Paintings by Cornwallis Harris in 1836 depict a white rhino above and a black rhino below. Note the soil colour variation as observed by the artist.

ABOVE: Note the variation in the skin tone due to the light falling on the rear rhino. Photo: Quintus Strauss.

LEFT: The author of this chapter, Jim Feely, demonstrates the action rhino take in when using tree trunks to rid themselves of ticks. Photo: Eric Thorburn.

and white rhino. Selous was fluent in Afrikaans, as no doubt were at least some of the others. He often accompanied Afrikaner hunters and would not have misunderstood them. However, one writer who did not use a common name was William Burchell, either in the original scientific description of *Rhinoceros simus* or in the account of his travels.

From this brief history, I believe it is clear that:

- The Dutch and Afrikaans name for C. simum has been wit(te)renoster since at least the end of the 18th century, as recorded by Barrow, Borcherds and Harris, and this is correctly translated as white rhino.
- The Dutch and Afrikaans name for *D. bicornis* gained the qualifier of 'swart' (black) at the same time as the other was named 'wit'.
- These names originated in the country inhabited by San, Griqua and Tswana north of the Orange River where both rhinos occurred together. By the late 18th century many Griqua were of mixed descent, as Barrow noted, and were bilingual speakers of Afrikaans and Khoekhoe. Consequently, it was probably they who were the first to use these names in Afrikaans and Dutch, as is suggested by Barrow's report.

Rookmaaker (2003) in his detailed study of the name 'white rhino' concluded, on the evidence quoted above that: 'The English adjective cannot have evolved from a Dutch or Afrikaans word. This derivation should no longer be used in popular texts to explain the name of the rhinoceros called "white".' By this he meant any Dutch or Afrikaans word except wit(te), from which it was translated. But he did think that the accounts of Barrow or Borcherds might 'hold the key to the truth', having also quoted the same passage in Borcherds's letter used here, although omitting that it was translated from Dutch.

Southwards of the Orange River, the black rhino continued to be known as just the renoster or rhinoster at least until 1841. Not long afterwards in 1853, or possibly 1858, the last of its kind in that region was killed near Port Elizabeth. This had been its name from the time when it was first encountered by the early Dutch settlers near Cape Town in the 17th century. They knew no other African rhino for more than a century thereafter that would have warranted distinguishing it specifically.

The names of the two species are a contrasting pair whether in Dutch and Afrikaans or in translation. As Teddy Roosevelt and E. Heller in 1915 said, 'The black rhinoceros has not received its common English name because its coloration is actually blacker than that of the other species, but rather to contrast it with the other African rhinoceros which has been so unfortunate as to have the designation "white" bestowed upon it.'

Since the names do not describe the skin colour of either species, they could allude metaphorically to their differing reactions to humans: swart referring to that species' well-known aggressiveness, with wit as its opposite for the inoffensive animal. Swart in Afrikaans and 'black' in English have similar metaphorical allusions to anger, danger or threat, as for instance in die swart kuns, swart kyk, 'the black art', 'things looked black', 'a black look'.[8] However, wit in Afrikaans does not have the allusions that 'white' has in English; in both languages they are just the opposites of swart or black.[9]

Behavioural differences between the two species

Thus, I would argue, the derivation of the name swart should be the issue with wit as its opposite, and not vice versa, as Roosevelt and Heller and most other writers have supposed. Nevertheless, there is neither etymological nor historical support for this idea. This difference must have been as significant to hunters of both rhinos as those in their outward appearance. In 1802 Somerville said of the black rhino, 'This animal is the most ferocious that Africa produces ... for when wounded he seldom fails to fly to the place from which the shot came.' Conversely, in mitigation, Borcherds at the same time wrote: 'One must surmise that much more is told of the ferociousness of this animal than is actually in his nature.'

A famous early report of black rhinos' bellicosity described Simon van der Stel's close encounter with one near Piketberg, in the present Western Cape in 1685. Alexander (1838) described this behavioural difference between the species: 'The white rhinoceros ... is a timid animal compared with the savage black, which commonly charges whether wounded or not, whereas the white variety tries to effect an escape.'

However, nine of the 10 etymological theories identified in the literature and discussed by Rookmaaker (2003) consider only the white rhino and its physical appearance, ignoring both the black and the behaviour of both. Borcherds's response to the name wit or white rhino in 1802 (quoted above) was echoed by nearly every writer after him. The earliest suggestion that the original Dutch and Afrikaans name for C. simum was not wit(te)renoster, and that another adjective had been misunderstood by English speakers, was a speculative proposal made in 1931 by Charles Pitman, first game warden of Uganda. At that time the northern white rhino (C.s. cottoni) still occurred in western Uganda, although it later became extinct there. He thought that a Dutch word meaning 'bright', 'shining' or 'great' might have been used instead of wit, but did not give an example of such use.

Thereafter the idea seems to have lain dormant in South Africa until revived by Charles Astley Maberly (1963) who wrote: 'There have been a variety of suggestions as to why the species became known as "white", the best I think being that offered by T.R.H. Owen – that it is a corruption of the term "wyd mond" or "broad-mouthed" originally applied by the old Boer hunters.'

The originally speculative suggestions of Pitman, Van den Bergh and Owen were clearly made in ignorance of the early 19th-century reports. They evolved into factoids in publications after 1963. These ignored the fact that no historical example of such a use had ever been produced in their support. And they went on being repeated, although not by Reay Smithers. He accepted my comments on his draft manuscript on the white rhino, omitted the speculation about the name, and relied on documented facts in *The Mammals of the Southern African Sub-region*, which became the standard work.

Short and pithy, swart or black with its opposite wit or white have remained firmly in everyday use for more than two centuries to distinguish the African rhinos. As a pair they are an appropriate metaphor in Afrikaans and English for a well-known difference in the rhinos' reactions to humans – at least today, if not used originally. Thus the names will no doubt continue in common usage, whatever their etymology or the alternatives preferred by zoologists.

One thing is certain, no other African animal
has attracted as much attention to its name as
has the white rhino.

CHAPTER 7

Living rhinos in today's world

The illegal wildlife trade threatens not only the survival of entire species, such as elephants and rhinos, but also the livelihoods and, often, the very lives of millions of people across Africa who depend on tourism for a living.

– YAYA TOURE, COTE D'IVOIRE FOOTBALL STAR

The five living rhino species[1]

The word 'rhinoceros' is derived from the Greek words ρινος, rhino, referring to the nose and kepac, the animal's horn hence 'horned-nose'. The plural can be rhinoceri, rhinoceroses, rhinoceroi or, in our case, rhinoceros. They are generally known as rhinos, which is the term we will most often use going forward – 'rhinoceros', with due respect, becomes a bit of a mouthful after continual use.

There are five living species of rhino (two in Africa; three in Asia):

- The white rhino (*Ceratotherium simum*) is one of the two African species, belonging to the Dicerotini group and entering the scene some 3 million years ago.

- The black rhino (*Diceros bicornis*) is the second African species, also belonging to the Dicerotini group. It first appeared in the middle Miocene period, 4 million years ago, making it one of the most stable and long-lived species on the African savannah. This fact in itself is more than good enough reason to ensure its survival.

- The Sumatran rhino (*Dicerorhinus sumartrensis*) is the first of the Asian species and is considered the oldest and most archaic form. It first appeared in the fossil record in the lower Miocene Epoch 20–16 million years ago. The Sumatran rhino, as we know it today, appeared about 2.5 million years ago.

- The Javan rhino (*Rhinoceros sundaicus*) is also Asian, and appeared approximately 2 million years ago.

- The greater one-horned rhino (*Rhinoceros unicornis*) is also Asian, appearing about 2 million years ago.

OPPOSITE: Black rhinoceros are browsers and eat a wide range of plants including certain poisonous varieties. Photo: Bruno Zanzottera.

PREVIOUS SPREAD: A female white rhinoceros and her very young calf. Without our urgent help they face a bleak future. Photo: WRSA/Quintus Strauss.

Comparison of the five remaining species of rhino[2]

We would like to attempt to clear up one aspect about the African rhino that has been the topic of much discussion since before the turn of the 19th century – and that is the question of the term white and black used to describe the separate species. In the true sense neither are black nor white, which frankly is a misnomer of the true definition of colour, for there is not that much to distinguish them by colour. From our own personal experience of working with both species, the black rhino more often appears slightly darker. The colour of both species, however, is due to their nature of frequently using mud wallows, taking on the appearance of the local soil. This is best summed up by Jim Feely – my mentor and guide on my first-ever training wilderness trail in Imfolozi in 1975 – in Chapter 6, 'Black rhino, white rhino – what's in a name?' Jim writes:

Short and pithy, swart or black with its opposite wit or white have remained firmly in everyday use for more than two centuries to distinguish the African rhinos. Thus the name will no doubt continue in common usage, whatever their etymology or the alternatives preferred by zoologists. One thing is certain, no African animal has attracted as much attention to its name as has the white rhino.

The white rhinoceros (*Ceratotherium simum*)

OTHER NAMES

Square-lipped rhinoceros

STATUS

Threatened

ESTIMATED NUMBER/LOCATION

The white rhinos' numbers are estimated to be between 19 682 and 21 077.[3]

Their former range extended over much of South Africa with the exception of the southern and eastern Cape, parts of Namibia, Botswana and Angola. Both Zimbabwe and Mozambique had good habitat. With the exception of the last surviving population in the bushveld of Zululand, they were totally exterminated by the turn of the 19th century. Mozambique had the dubious distinction of having the species go extinct twice.rThe northern white rhinoceros (*Ceratotherium simum cottoni*) was formerly found in north-western Uganda, southern Chad, south-

White rhinoceros are grazers and may weigh up to 3 000 kilograms. Photo: WRSA/ Quintus Strauss.

TOP: The spoor (track) of a white rhino. Photo: Clive Walker.

BOTTOM: Fungi growing amidst the dung of a white rhinoceros. Photo: Clive Walker.

western Sudan, the eastern parts of the Central African Republic and north-eastern Democratic Republic of Congo. They are now extinct.

DESCRIPTION

Second only in size to the African elephant, they can attain a shoulder height of up to 1.8 metres (6 ft). They weigh up to 3 000 kilograms (6 600 lbs), have a large head with a broad chest and a short neck. They have a massive 'nuchal' hump on their shoulders supporting the large head and short, stocky, powerful legs. In spite of their size, they are swift-running animals, reaching speeds up to 40 km/h.

THE HORNS

Both male and female carry two horns on their snout, which are defensive weapons. They are not attached directly to the skull and are generally much larger and heavier than the remaining four extant species of rhino. The horns, as in the case of the extinct woolly rhino, the black rhino and the three Asian rhino, are made of keratin, which is the same type of protein that makes up hair and fingernails. Should a rhino break off its horn or is dehorned for whatever reason, it will regrow at the rate of about 10 cm per year.

The white rhino skull weight is 15.1 kg plus the lower jaw of 6.6 kg 21.7 kg (compared to the black rhino of 10.9 kg plus lower jaw 5.8 kg 16.7 kg).

One of the first white rhino introduced to Lapalala Wilderness in 1982 broke off its beautiful anterior (front) horn at the base while in transit from Zululand (KwaZulu). Over the ensuing years the horn steadily grew back, but was never the same graceful shape. At the time of her death many years later when she and her calf were killed outright by a lightning bolt, the horn was massive and bulky.

BEHAVIOUR/HABITS/HABITAT

Their daily habits have been observed as spending time feeding, preferably in open savanna, wallowing in mud or dust bowls, and sleeping or resting.

Never underestimate their supposedly docile nature. They do not take kindly to being held in enclosures when first captured and are fast and potentially extremely dangerous. The black rhino by contrast can display a ferocious nature and generally is the opposite when captured, calming down far more easily.

Much of the demise of the species in southern Africa during the 19th century was attributed to their regular habits and the advantage to well-mounted hunters (on horseback) for their docile nature. Unlike the black rhino, they are in most cases happy to run away, although instances of determined white rhino attacks on walking trails in South Africa have resulted in injury to participants and in some cases death to the rhino. No one should ever underestimate these creatures and the one lesson we were taught over and over was that if we had to shoot a rhino for whatever reason, we should seriously consider shooting ourselves! Fortunately, in the 18 years we conducted trails in rhino country, none of our officers ever had to kill a rhino in self-defence. To be fair, each incident needs to be judged on merit and there may very well be reason for an attack, although this is rare.

Apart from oxpeckers, the same role of tick removal is taken over by terrapins in mud wallows. Broken tree stumps make excellent rubbing posts that keep their skin healthy and also help to remove parasites. As with all rhino, their skins are thick and tough, which is one of the reasons why they were hunted for hides and meat. If the animal is not fatally wounded, the skin closes over the entry wound and later causes serious infection, invariably leading to its death. Today's modern rifles, which are more often used in poaching, fire light-calibre bullets, leaving even smaller openings.

Their dung can occur almost anywhere in quite large piles from single animals or the accumulations of a few individuals, and can often be seen in large communal middens.

DIET/DUNG

They are grass-eaters, preferring open areas. Their dung usually turns quite dark in colour with age.

THE SENSES

Their eyesight is poor beyond 30 metres, relying as they do on their excellent hearing and highly developed sense of smell. Birds are an early-warning system for them, especially both species of oxpecker.

MATING/GESTATION

A single calf is born after a gestation period of around 18 months. The calf remains with the mother for up to three years, generally proceeding the mother when walking, as opposed to that of the black rhino which precedes the mother.

COMMUNICATION

They have a wide range of vocal sounds from squeaks, squeals, growls to grunts, and on occasion a plaintive cry.

TOP: Both species of rhino are very fond of rolling in mud to cool themselves and to thwart biting flies. Photo: Clive Walker.

BOTTOM: The characteristic curved tail of a white rhinoceros. Photo: WRSA.

The black rhinoceros (*Diceros bicornis*)

OTHER NAMES

English: *hooked-lipped rhinoceros*

Afrikaans: *swartrenoster*

Zulu/isiNdebele: *ubejane*

Northern Sotho/Tswana: *tshukudu*

Xhosa: *ummkhombe*

Venda: *thema*

Herero: *ngara*

Tsonga: *mhelembe*

Kung San/Khi Shona: *chipenbere, nhema*

Lozi: *sukulu*

Yei: *unsunguzu*

Nama/Damara: *!Nabas*

Swahili: *faro*

STATUS

Critically Endangered

ESTIMATED NUMBER/LOCATION

The black rhinos' numbers are estimated to be between 5 420 and 5 455.[4]

There are only four subspecies of black rhino surviving in Africa today in only four countries, with significant populations in sub-Saharan countries, with the exception of the tropical rain zones:

- South-central black rhino (*Diceros bicornis minor*), the most numerous, which once ranged from central Tanzania south through Zambia, Zimbabwe, Mozambique, Malawi, Botswana to north and south-eastern South Africa.
- South-western black rhino (*Diceros bicornis bicornis*) from southern Angola, western Botswana, north-western Cape, extending as far south as the Cape Peninsula, including Addo and the Karoo.
- Eastern black rhino (*Diceros bicornis michaeli*) once ranged from South Sudan to central Tanzania, but today they are largely confined to Kenya.
- The West African subspecies (*Diceros bicornis longipes*) is generally considered extinct.

The black rhino during the 20th century was considered the most numerous of all the five extant species of rhino. At the turn of the 19th century, there were conceivably several hundred thousand living throughout their range. During the latter half of the 20th century, their numbers were between 65 000 and 100 000. Between 1960 and 1980 these numbers plummeted to around 15 000 as a result of severe poaching. The advent of conflict and tribal warfare saw the arrival of the most effective and relatively cheap military weapon ever manufactured, the AK-47, firing a small, inexpensive bullet.

TOP LEFT: The scrape marks of a black rhino. Photo: Clive Walker.

TOP RIGHT: Rocks used by black rhinoceros in arid zones in Namibia. Photo: Clive Walker.

BOTTOM: A mud-covered black rhinoceros browsing in a holding pen. Photo: Clive Walker.

TOP: The skull of a black rhinoceros. The length of the skull is much less than that of white rhinoceros. Photo: Clive Walker.

LEFT: The spoor of the black rhinoceros. Photo: Clive Walker.

ABOVE: Dung beetles are constantly in attendance with fresh dung. Photo: Clive Walker.

DESCRIPTION

The black rhino is smaller than the white, standing between 1.4 and 1.7 metres high (55–67 inches) at the shoulder, and a length between 3.3 and 3.6 metres (11–12 ft). They weigh between 800 and 1 400 kg (1 800–3 100 lbs). The head, which is much smaller than the white rhino, is held high. The females are smaller than the males, but both are extremely swift, reaching speeds of up to 56 km/h. They are capable of turning rapidly and are extremely agile.

THE HORNS

Both male and female carry two horns on the end of their snout, which are not attached directly to the skull. The horns, as in the case of the extinct woolly rhino, the white rhino and the three Asian rhino, are made up of keratin – the same type of protein that makes up human hair or fingernails. Should a rhino break off its horn, or is dehorned for whatever reason, it will regrow at the rate of 6–10 cm (or 750 g/year). This is subject, of course, to normal wear through rubbing, and varies according to the individual animal's behaviour and environment.

In the case of the eastern black rhino (*D.b.michaeli*), historically they have always been known to carry longer, more slender-tapered horns than the other two subspecies. According to Rowland Ward, in *Records of Big Game*, the longest horn

The third longest horn of a black rhinoceros on record. Photo: Peter Jenkins Archive.

recorded at 120 cm came from Tanzania and one by R. Finch, in Kenya, measured 119.3 cm. The black rhino horn that was hunted and removed by Eric Rundgren, former Kenyan professional hunter, is believed to be the third-longest on record taken on safari near Mt Kenya.

It is interesting to note that Brian Hearn, one of Kenya's renowned professional hunters, comments in his book *White Hunter* that back in the 1970s, when Kenya's rhino population was estimated to be in the order of 20 000, most professional hunters of good repute would not take a rhino with a horn unless it was between 46 and 51 cm (18–20 inches). He furthermore noted that the hunting fraternity in 1972 purchased only 34 licences and only 19 animals were actually shot. That year alone Hong Kong's official records revealed that 1 000 rhino horns were imported from Kenya. We know only too well what transpired in East Africa thereafter.

The south-western black rhino (*D.b.bicornis*) often possess long, thick, flat-shaped horns with occasionally the anterior horn exceeding the front horn. They are the largest of the three subspecies of rhino in terms of body size. The south-central black rhino (*D.b.minor*) carries far smaller and more slender horns, and they are the smallest in body size of the three subspecies.

The weight of a black rhino skull is 10.9 kg plus the lower jaw of 5.8 kg 16.7 kg (as opposed to that of the white rhino: 15.1 kg plus the lower jaw of 6.6 kg 21.7 kg).

BEHAVIOUR/HABITS/HABITAT

Black rhino tend to be solitary by nature with strong bonds between mother and calf (for new observations, see Chapter 5 about monitoring the black rhino in SANParks). Both males and females have a reputation for being extremely aggressive. They will charge if they feel they are threatened and this may have a lot to do with their poor eyesight causing them to panic and become confused. They are an extremely misunderstood animal – I believe few zoology students choose to study them out of fear – but their reputation is undeserved and those who have had the privilege of working with wild and captive black rhinos will testify to this fact.

Contrary to popular belief that they are stupid, they are intelligent creatures. They communicate with one another at a level inaudible to humans, are generally solitary by nature but will interact with one another on occasion, and do not possess good eyesight which causes them to be curious about strange sounds if they do not detect the disturbance by scent. Their habit of 'attack' is, I believe, a defence mode. However, large African animals should always be looked upon as potentially dangerous – it does not necessarily mean they are bad tempered or 'stupid', 'dumb' or 'brutish'. Unfortunately, they carry a great deal of baggage, largely from ill-informed travellers and hunters who became writers, especially during the 19th century and into the early part of the 20th century.

Dangerous? The dictionary describes the word as: A thing that causes peril or exposure to harm. There is no doubt the animal *can* be frightfully dangerous and the only reason more people are killed by elephant in Africa every year is because elephants number in their tens of thousands and the black rhino is so frighteningly low in numbers.

Black rhino are also mainly active by night and will do anything to avoid human scent or sight. If you happen to walk into a slumbering rhino and disturb it, it will in most instances run away, but it may also rapidly spin around through 180 degrees. If it smells, hears and sees you, it may well charge directly at you. Much may have to do with poor eyesight, but we are inclined to believe the animal's natural reaction is one of defensiveness. If it has only smelled you, it may stand with head held fully erect, facing the direction of the perceived threat, sniffing and listening, with ears rotating. A loud snort may then herald a charge with the head slightly lowered, accelerating with constant 'huffing'. They are also able to turn rapidly and are extremely agile and, unlike the elephant, they are capable of jumping.

A black rhinoceros in a holding pen in Zululand. Note the blood-encrusted lesions which one encounters in animals from this region. Photo: Clive Walker.

Never go walking in any area where rhinos occur unless with an experienced tracker. If on foot and pursued by one, you may with some considerable effort dodge it at the last moment, but that is certainly not your best option. What you need to do is get up a tree immediately, regardless of the thorns, making certain it is pretty stout, for if sufficiently riled the rhino may pound the tree with horn or chest and may even leap up to dislodge you. There are few experiences that can arrest the mind so effectively – so when walking, make a mental note to observe trees around nearby you, and in the event of a charge, aim for that tree. Do not turn around and run – you will never outrun a rhino!

Black rhinos are browsers, which accounts for their habitat preference of dense bush, using their prehensile lip and horn to good effect. They are particularly fond of mud wallows and will spend lengthy periods lying up, keeping their body temperature down. The mud is of importance to the health of the animal's skin, as well as for warding off biting flies. In the absence of mud, they will happily wallow in dust bowls. The thick skin is sparsely coated in bristly hairs; they have fringes of hair around their ears and a tuft of dark hair on the tail. Skin lesions occur in certain populations caused by a filarial parasite and may be found on the front upper body parts and on the flank behind the shoulder. These lesions are blood encrusted, and they ulcerate and haemorrhage – to the uninitiated they may appear as a nasty wound. When the animal is translocated to areas not affected by the 'fly', they disappear.

The adults normally have no natural enemies other than humans intent on killing them for their horns.

DIET/DUNG

Black rhinos eat a wide range of plants – twigs, branches, leafy plants, forbs and shoots. Up to 220 plants have been recorded, including certain poisonous varieties. They will use their horn to pull down branches and will also use their chest to push over small trees to reach twigs and foliage. They will drink daily, consuming as much as 30 litres and are capable of going for many days without water if the drinking locations are widely spaced, as with the rhino in the arid zones of Namibia.

They usually defecate in middens or along various routes, and the dung is scattered with the hind legs. It is easily identified by its fibrous and woody nature, containing twigs that have clipped ends owing to the way the pre-molar teeth bite them (with a shearing rather than a grinding action). It is a lighter colour than that of the white rhino.

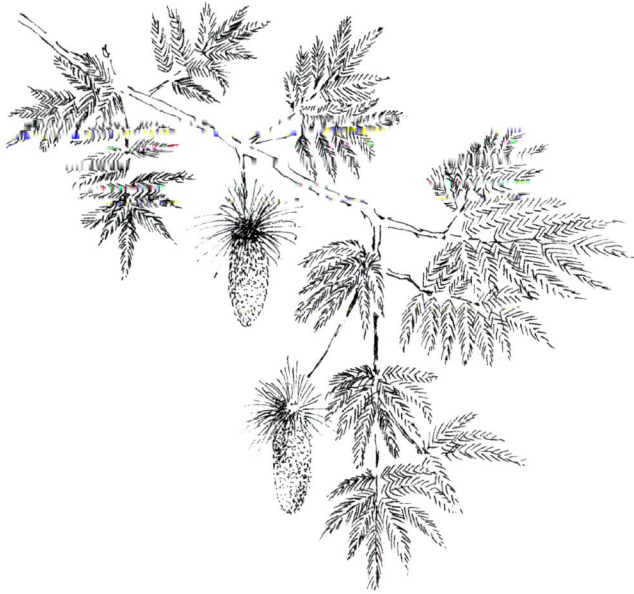

THE SENSES

Their eyesight is poor beyond 30 metres, but their motion detection is good up to 60 metres. Their sense of hearing and smell are excellent, and their ears have a wide, rotational range enabling them to detect sound. If observed lying down, seemingly asleep, you will notice the ears constantly rotating. Birds are their best warning of danger, especially both species of oxpecker, the red-billed (*Buphagus erythrorhynchus*) and the yellow-billed (*Buphagus africanus*). These birds will instantly raise the alarm at the approach of any danger. They fly off, immediately alerting the rhino with a loud, hissing call. Another ally is the fork-tailed drongo (*Dicrurus adsimilis*), a noisy and aggressive bird.

MATING/GESTATION

A single calf is born, weighing between 35 and 50 kilograms at birth after a gestation period of between 15 and 16 months at any time of the year. Courtship involves a series of complex encounters between the bull and the cow. According to Smithers 1983, 'The bull approaches her circumspectly in a stiff-legged gait, his hind legs dragging on the ground, and face to face they spar with their front horns or they nudge each other with the sides of their heads.' Courtship can last for several hours with the bull mounting the cow frequently. After successful copulation, which may take up to 30 minutes or sometimes longer, the bull and cow both remain silent.[5]

The calf is weaned at around two years and remains with the mother for up to three years. This can be a very vulnerable period for calves from other males wishing to mate with the mother. They have the highest rates in combat-related encounters

ABOVE: Black rhinoceros copulating in the arid zone regions of Namibia. Photo: STRTrust.

LEFT: Other than humans, the lion is a potential predator of young rhino. Photo: Clive Walker.

of any mammal, with deaths being recorded in both sexes. Calves may be killed or seriously injured during these contacts, as well as the threat of possible predation by hyenas or lions. Black rhino mothers are known to be extremely aggressive at this time and will endeavour to protect the calf vigorously

The calf generally follows the mother, as opposed to that of the white rhino, which walks ahead.

COMMUNICATION

Black rhino have a wide range of vocal sounds, which they use to communicate to one another, and they have a few sounds to express their displeasure. Long snorts with the attendant swift expelling of air may indicate anger or danger of an approaching threat. Erect ears will be a sign that the animal is trying to locate the source of the intruder, followed by ears pressed flat back if responding aggressively. In the event of a charge, they are capable of attaining a top speed in a very short distance and on the point of contact will propel with their head up with incredible speed and force by means of the very powerful neck and shoulder muscles.

DISTINGUISHING FEATURES OF BLACK AND WHITE RHINO[6]

FEATURE	BLACK RHINO	WHITE RHINO
Size	Smaller	Larger
Lip shape	Upper lip overhangs lower and is pointed and prehensile for browsing	Upper lip does not overhang lower and is square for grazing
Head/neck length	Head length less than the neck length	Head length more than the neck length
Neckline	Slightly convex, almost straight	Pronounced convex nuchal hump
Tail position	Straight and horizontal when defecating, alarmed or running	Curled when defecating or running; horizontal when standing and alarmed
Ear shape	Tip rounded	Tip pointed
Calf position when on the move	Calf follows mother	Calf proceeds mother
Carriage of head	Lower jaw usually horizontal to the ground or angled to browse	Lower jaw always below the horizontal; mouth mostly just above the ground to graze

The Sumatran rhinoceros (Dicerorhinus sumatrensis)

A Sumatran rhinoceros, the smallest of the three Asian rhino species. Photo: IRF-US.

OTHER NAMES

The hairy rhinoceros

STATUS

Critically Endangered

ESTIMATED NUMBER/LOCATION

The Sumatran rhinos' numbers are estimated to be 76.[7] It is believed to be extinct in the wild in Malaysia (Peninsula and Sabah), and is restricted to only four isolated sites in Indonesia with as many as 10 subpopulations. Three animals survive in Kalimantan (Borneo).

Only six substantial populations exist, four on Sumatra, one in Borneo and one in the Malay Peninsula. The population trend is down from the original estimated number of 200 individuals. In 2015 the minimum total number was estimated less than 100.[8]

The difficulty in determining numbers is due to the shy nature of the animal and the dense, sometimes mountainous, rainforest in which they reside, and added to that is the limited effort and the expenditure. It is easy to imagine what working in these tropical conditions must be like.

DESCRIPTION

This is the smallest of all the rhinos, standing about 1.20–1.45 metres (3.9–4.76 ft) at the shoulder, weighing between 500 and 800 kilograms (1 100– 1 800 lbs). It has two horns, and the body is largely covered in reddish-brown hair, the skin being relatively thin.

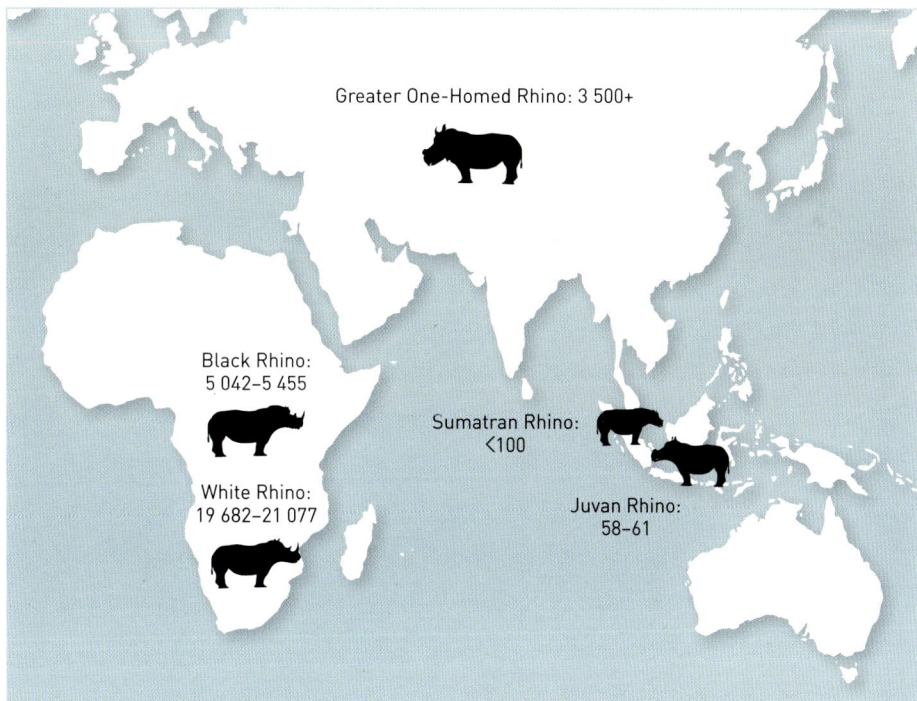

Greater One-Horned Rhino: 3 500+

Black Rhino:
5 042–5 455

White Rhino:
19 682–21 077

Sumatran Rhino:
<100

Juvan Rhino:
58–61

THE HORNS

The animal carries two horns, 15–25 cm (5.9–9.8 inches).

BEHAVIOUR/HABITS/HABITAT

Of all the rhino the Sumatran is the most vocal.

It is agile and quick, easily climbing mountains, steep slopes, ravines and riverbanks. They are very good swimmers taking full advantage one would imagine of riverine and aquatic vegetation. Being shy and solitary, they do not appear to defend territories through fighting and appear somewhat docile.

They prefer dense, sometimes mountainous, rainforest, and once inhabited the rain and cloud forests and swamps in India, Bhutan, Laos, Bangladesh, Myanmar, Thailand, Malaysia, Indonesia and China. Human expansion over time, and especially in China, played a major role in their decline and the extinction of both the Javan and Sumatran rhinos ... apart from poaching activities for the horn.

DIET

Sumatran rhinos are browsers.

THE SENSES

They have a good sense of smell and hearing, but are rather short sighted.

MATING/GESTATION

Females are sexually mature at four years and the males at seven years. The gestation period is approximately 15–16 months.

COMMUNICATION

These rhinos are surprisingly vocal with their whistling and whining.

The Javan rhinoceros (Rhinoceros sondaicus sondaicus)

The Javan rhinoceros are the rarest of all the five extant species of rhino. Photo: IRF-US.

OTHER NAMES

Lesser one-horned rhinoceros

STATUS

Critically Endangered

ESTIMATED NUMBER/LOCATION

The Javan rhinos' numbers are estimated to be 60 to 63.[9] It is likely there are no more than this number surviving. Once the most widespread of all the Asian species from India, throughout Southeast Asia, the islands of Indonesia and China, they only exist today in one population in the Ujung Kulon National Park on the island of West Java, Indonesia.

TOP AND BOTTOM: A female Sumatran rhinoceros with her young captive-bred calf. Photos: International Rhino Foundation.

It is the most critically endangered of the five extant species of rhino and is probably the rarest large mammal on Earth. According to the African Rhino Specialist Group (AfRSG), having all individuals in one single location is a strategic risk, leaving them vulnerable to poaching, volcanic activity or a major tsunami, as well as the potential of being infected by disease-bearing domestic cattle. Plans, over decades, to create a second population have not materialised.

DESCRIPTION

A solitary animal, standing at a height of 3.1–3.2 metres (10–10.5 ft), it is second in size only to the white rhino. Their weight is between 900 and 2 300 kilograms (2 000–5 060 lbs). The species belongs to the same genus as the greater one-horned rhino and has a similar likeness in terms of its armour-plated appearance. It is hairless with grey-brown skin, falling in folds to the shoulder, back and rump. The neck folds are less conspicuous than those in the greater one-horned species. The life span is approximately 30–45 years.

THE HORN

They carry a single horn that may grow to about 25 cm (10 inches).

BEHAVIOUR/HABITS/HABITAT

As with all rhino, they are very fond of wallowing, which enables them to control their body temperature, and keeps the skin free of disease and parasites. They are a solitary and shy animal but can demonstrate aggression when approached.

DIET

A browser, eating a wide range of plants, twigs, shoots, fruit and foliage, they consume up to 50 kilograms (110 lbs) of food daily. Salt is an important aspect of the diet.

THE SENSES

The Javan rhinos have a good sense of smell and hearing, but are rather short sighted.

GESTATION

The gestation period is from 16–19 months.

COMMUNICATION

They are not very vocal.

The greater one-horned rhinoceros (Rhinoceros unicornis)

The readily recognised 'armour' plating of the greater one-horned rhinoceros, also known as the Indian rhinoceros. Photo: Clive Walker.

Also called the Indian rhinoceros or the Asian one-horned rhinoceros. In German, they are called *Panzer nashorn* (translated as 'tank').

STATUS

Endangered

ESTIMATED NUMBER/LOCATION

The greater one-horned rhinos' numbers are estimated to be 3 550 plus and these are improving.[10]

Is it a good idea or not to mention rhino numbers of any given area due to the high demand for horn? South Africa today avoids totals for specific parks. In the case of the Asian species, this is difficult due to the very low surviving numbers and as in the case of this species, there are only two viable populations. There is a tendency to think poachers don't read papers, listen to radios, watch television or access the internet. How wrong can one be – as we have come to realise only too painfully in South Africa. So the less you say the better ... US$60 000 (±R810 000) per kilo for a horn is a staggering amount (and when you think that people in South Africa are sometimes killed just for their cellphones).

These rhino once ranged over a vast area of the entire northern part of the Indian subcontinent, from Pakistan in the west to the Indian–Burmese border, including parts of Nepal, Bangladesh and Bhutan. Their presence was also possible in southern China, Indo-China and Myanmar (Burma), according to the literature. Today they are extinct in most parts of their former range and are confined largely to areas that are surrounded by human-dominated landscapes that are not fenced, which results in them wandering into these areas, rendering them vulnerable to poaching.

In the two countries that today still have viable populations of these rhino, the bulk are to be found in Kaziranga National Park in Assam, Manas National Park, Pabitora Wildlife Sanctuary and Orang National Park in India, as well as in Nepal's Chitwan National Park and Bardiar National Park.

The Elimination of Malaria Programme from 1954 was so successful that by 1960 the area was declared malaria-free, resulting in thousands of 'hill people' pouring into the region, which set about the inevitable destruction of the habitat. A great deal of the credit for the ultimate establishment of Chitwan National Park must go to the Fauna Preservation Society and the International Union for the Conservation of Nature (IUCN). Creating the park was no easy matter and required the removal of over 22 000 locals in 1964, which was met at the time with a great deal of resentment – something that would be extremely difficult today.

Approval to establish the park was made by the late King Mahendra in 1970. It is a real plus when the head of state is on your side. Royal Chitwan National Park was officially gazetted in 1973, becoming the first national park in Nepal. It came just in time to save the rhino and what was left of the Chitwan Forest, having by then lost two-thirds forever. Moves to establish the park were largely due to the serious decline of the rhino and other species of wildlife as evidenced by a survey produced by GH Caughley and HR Mishra, estimating there were between 81 and 108 rhino. Tough choices had to be made: 'Are rhinos more important than people?' In this case the answer was 'yes', given the past history of slaughter. Chitwan today is the second-most important sanctuary conserving the species in Asia.

LEFT: The greater one-horned rhinoceros are good swimmers, happy to remain close to water. Photo: Clive Walker.

TOP RIGHT: The best and possibly only way to view the Indian rhinoceros is atop the back of a riding elephant. The grass – as one can see – often exceeds the height of the elephant. Photo: Clive Walker.

The Indian population has benefitted greatly from the support of the UK-based Save the Rhino International organisation and the US-based International Rhino Foundation.

DESCRIPTION

The greater one-horned rhino is second only in size to the African white rhino, weighing in at between 2 200 and 3 000 kilograms (4 900 and 6 600 lbs). They attain a height of between 1.7 and 2 metres (5 ft 7 inches and 6 ft 7 inches), and are taller than the white rhino. The skin is a silver-brown colour, becoming pinkish near the large skin folds that cover the body. These folds are especially well developed in males, giving them the appearance of armour plating. The name for them in German is *Panzer nashorn* (translated as 'tank'). No other member of the rhino family comes remotely near this species in terms of its appearance, which could justify the title of 'prehistoric'.

THE HORN

A single horn is present in both sexes – the horn of the three Asian rhino being far more valuable than the African rhinos'. A great deal of credit for their survival lies with the international NGOs who have assisted the authorities, as well as the dedication of the staff of the various parks.

The most prized and the greatest value of all the body parts of a rhino is its horn. Esmond Bradley Martin, recognised trade specialist, in a report first published in 1981, noted that the Chinese regarded the horn of this rhino as the best of all the rhino species. But there is very little of a rhino carcass in general that is not coveted for some purpose or other in Southeast Asia. In instances of poaching when a weapon is used, there is little wasted time other than to remove the horn as quickly as possible and to vanish. According to KK Gurung, when a rhino died from natural causes or disease and the authorities had authorised the villagers to remove the body, the rush to get at the carcass often resulted in knife wounds.

The usages are varied and to a 'Westerner' some make for compelling reading. Virtually every body part will have a use: blood for menstrual problems and excessive bleeding after childbirth; urine as a remedy for asthma, stomach pains and tuberculosis; dung as a laxative and mixed with tobacco and smoked cures coughs; the skin is highly sought after; and the meat, even if stinking and covered in maggots, is consumed with relish.

BEHAVIOUR/HABITS/HABITAT

They have the attributes of both black and white rhino combined with a few extra points in their favour. They are excellent swimmers, happy to wallow and feed in lakes, streams, rivers and mud pools. The problem for this species is that the parks that hold them are not fenced and they are in effect 'islands' in a sea of humanity. Apart from poaching, the greatest threat is from wandering into adjacent farmland causing damage. They can also be a potential threat to humans, and have been known to kill people, although generally speaking they are a reasonably placid creature compared to the black rhino.

In the 1980s, certainly in Chitwan where they were so plentiful, they became a positive menace to farmers surrounding the park. The species enjoyed special protection, which included the added benefit of the presence of the Nepalese army. The Maoist uprising from 1996–2005 resulted in the decline of the military presence, leading to the slaughter of many of the park's rhino. Fortunately the position has much improved.

DIET

They are primarily grazers, but are known to eat leaves, branches of shrubs and trees, agricultural crops and fruit, as well as submerged and floating vegetation, plunging their heads under the water for up to 45 seconds.

THE SENSES

These rhinos have a good sense of smell and hearing, but are rather short sighted.

MATING/GESTATION

Females are sexually mature at around four years and males at around nine years. The gestation is approximately 15–16 months. They live for up to 30–45 years.

COMMUNICATION

They have 12 different sounds, including snorts, honks and roars.

When reading this chapter, it is clear that all three Asian species were numerous and once enjoyed a vast range. Hunting for the horn has been the major cause of their decline, but, by the same token, human expansion has had a disastrous effect. It is highly unlikely they could ever have hoped to retain their geographical range in the environment we face today, even if the horn was worthless. Added to the complexities of the Asian belief in traditional medicine (TCM), which goes back thousands of years, is it any wonder they are now at such alarmingly low levels?

Fortunately for the rhino it is easier to raise funds for their survival from a concerned public as they are mega fauna 'superstars' than it would be, for instance, the Thai python. That poor animal ends up being skinned alive and hung up like Monday washing in order not to damage the skin, the product ending up in luxury shoes, belts and handbags in the capitals of the world. There is, of course, one fundamental difference: the rhino is a keystone species and if we cannot ensure its survival, then in the end it may well be a barometer of our own survival. The real problem is we don't have many rhino left.

Will the world carry on if the rhino goes? Of course it will, and to be perfectly honest most of humanity knows very little about them or cares very much if they do disappear.

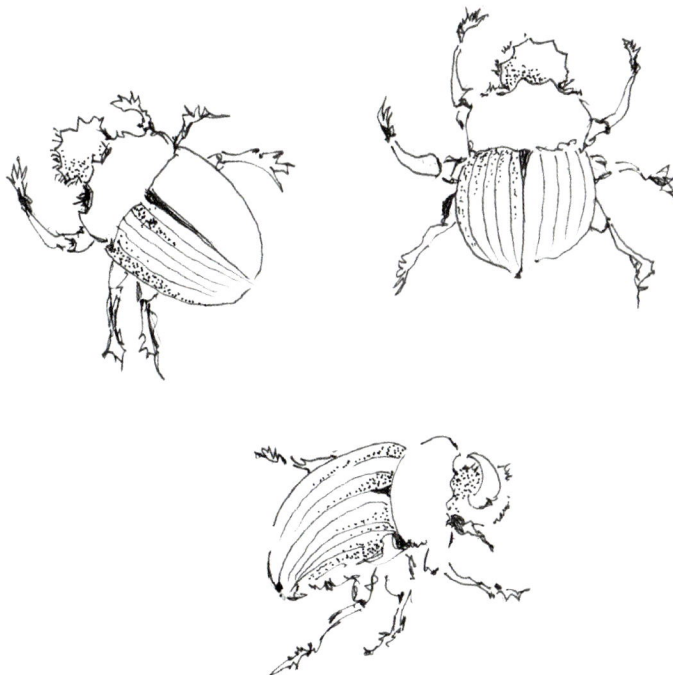

ENDANGERED WILDLIFE JOURNEY FOR CLIVE AND ANTON

In 1984, Anton and I undertook a trip that centred around endangered wildlife, starting in Mauritius to learn more about the conservation of the Mauritian kestrel and the pink pigeon, both highly threatened, as well as the opportunity to view a skeleton of the extinct dodo preserved in a glass case. We were also fortunate to spend two weeks in India and Nepal, and on our list was a visit to Kaziranga National Park and the Corbett Tiger Sanctuary. However, the assassination of the prime minister of India, Indira Ghandi, the week of our departure put the country into a state of turmoil and resulted in widespread deaths and burning of vehicles driven mainly by unfortunate Sikhs (the assassin was in fact a Sikh himself). Unfortunately, this resulted in our itinerary being altered and we were unable to visit that particular park and sanctuary.

The population of India was at that time around 800 million (it is now closer to 1.2 billion). With population levels of those proportions, where today half of its children are undernourished and half the population live below the international poverty level of less than US$1.25 a day, how does one hope to ensure the survival of the greater one-horned rhino or the Bengal tiger? My own awareness of the plight of the tiger goes back to 1973 when the first international campaign was launched to save the species, and then again in 2011. The rhino falls into the same category – perhaps not with the same fanfare as the tiger – but the demand for the horn is much worse. As economies accelerate alongside of massive population growth, the demand increases, ensuring both mega species remain highly endangered. Some 33 years later, in spite of the population explosion, the tiger and rhino are happily still with us. Sadly, though, one of the tiger sanctuaries we visited had a population of 30 tigers in 1984 and today they are extinct.

Sport hunting back in the 1800s most certainly played a role in the decline of the rhino, similar to South Africa. One English sportsman, Colonel Fitzwilliam Thomas Pollock slaughtered no less than 47 rhino in Assam, and in Bengal the Maharajah of Cooch Behar outdid himself by shooting 207 over a period 26 years. In 1896 the Bengal government was paying bounty hunters 20 rupees for every rhino shot. Worse still was the clearing of prime rhino habitat to establish tea plantations.

Tigers may well kill young rhino and, once again, represent the rhino's only prey other than man. Photo: Brian Courtney.

What is nevertheless startling is that India today has some 500 sanctuaries and 13 biospheres. International funding comes from various quarters and there is a high awareness at various levels. The diversity of wildlife of the Indian sub-continent is astonishing and is deserving of every bit of support and encouragement. But not unlike southern Africa, the question that begs asking is: 'How well are they run in terms of staff, and is there the concomitant funding to adequately conserve these areas and their species in the face of pervasive and ecologically devastating human encroachment?'

Having been unsuccessful in visiting Kaziranga National Park and the Corbett Tiger Sanctuary due to the violence, we headed north to Katmandu from Delhi, gateway to the Himalayas and the jungles of Chitwan (meaning 'heart of the jungle'). We visited Nepal's most famous park, Chitwan National Park, home to the greater one-horned rhino and some 40 tigers. There are a few ways of getting around Chitwan – one that Anton and I chose was from the back of an elephant (the last time I'd done that was in the Johannesburg zoo at the age of six). The size of the elephant will determine the number it will carry, and for the next two days we split the group up over five elephants. We duly set out each morning and afternoon with the attendant mahouts in search of rhino, swaying in tune with the elephant's gait. The grass through which the elephant trust their individual ways is incredibly tall, showing no fear of the rhino – when you do see them they don't appear big at all, being observed from more than two metres above the jungle floor.

Depending on which mahout sees a rhino first, he whistles to his colleagues who immediately turn their elephants towards his. Caution is taken not to crowd the rhino as they have been known to charge – fortunately this is rare.

We later spent three days on foot jungle-trekking with Dan Bahada, an expert jungle guide, and four porters, carrying the one-man tents, food (mainly rice), and four live chickens in a bamboo cage, slung across a porter's back. This part of Chitwan consisted of tall forest, rising up more than 40 metres, often closing at the top shutting out the sunlight, while brilliantly coloured scarlet minivets (*Pericrocotus flammeus*) flitted in and out of the forest canopy. The birdlife of the Indian sub-continent is astonishing. Down below we followed jungle trails often in and out of dense vegetation. A host of species live here ... a tiger passed by our camp the first night, and we also came across a sloth bear (*Melursus ursinus*). Dan whispered that they can be unpredictable and nasty if they so choose. They weigh 136 kilograms (300 lbs) and have a distinctive 'V' or crescent on the chest set off by a shaggy, black coat. This one had his rear end up in the air furiously digging into a termite mound. We quietly left him to his task.

On our last day as we headed back to Tiger Tops Lodge, we encountered a large male greater one-horned rhino at close range. When you are on foot you are suddenly very conscious of their size, which is even more impressive given the body folds. There wasn't an awful lot of space between us, but Dan was unperturbed. The rhino was fortunately below us, busy feeding on bamboo in a densely wooded stream with more than half his body in water. We watched him for more than half an hour, close to the animal, and he had no idea of our presence. This reminded me of how easy they can be killed by hunters expert in their ways.

According to KK Gurung, who at the time of our visit was manager of the lodge, the rhino is a sacred animal in Nepal. There is much we don't realise about customs of other countries, imposing our beliefs on long-held traditions, which are most often the cause of confusion and misunderstanding.

It is necessary to pause here and think carefully when pronouncing our views on traditions that often go back a very long way.

Afterwords

Yolan Friedmann

The upsurge of rhino poaching across all range states since 2007 has become something of a modern conservation crisis on a number of levels. Naturally, for the rhino and for the long-term survival of this icon of the African wilderness, the loss of over 25% of the combined population of black and white rhino in just a decade signals a serious crisis and places a question mark on their ability to survive. But in many ways, the crisis runs deeper than that. Just as conservationists sprang into action when the trends in rhino poaching appeared to be changing at alarming rates, so began a rapid shift and, in many cases, a rapidly expanding divide in the landscape of conservation action, ideologies, interventions, perspectives, opinions, special interests and priority setting. Over the past decade, the rhino crisis has catapulted governments, civil society, wildlife owners, NGOs, biologists and politicians into a series of confrontations with one another and, I would suggest, with ourselves, with less than favourable or constructive outcomes.

The Endangered Wildlife Trust (EWT) has been actively working for the conservation of endangered species since its establishment by Clive Walker, Neville Anderson and James Clarke in 1973. For over 44 years, we have been at the forefront of addressing the threats to the conservation of the African wildlife that is heritage and home to us all. The role of the EWT as mediator, initiator and convenor has taught the Trust to understand and navigate its way around 'human nature' in order to arrive at a positive outcome. In recent times, the fate of the rhino, and a host of other species that are being equally decimated by rampant illegal trade and escalating greed, has suggested that 'human nature' will be the final test of all humanity – and not just the obstacle around which some of us must work.

Clive and Anton Walker have described in great detail and with extensive evidence the numerous tenets to the complexity of today's 'rhino crisis'. It is clear that the crisis faced by the rhino today cannot be solved with the solutions of yesterday. The 21st century presents criminal networks with high-tech weaponry that kills in larger numbers, sophisticated forms of communication, efficient transport systems to move product quickly, and more effective ways of corrupting people into networks. It has presented consumers with changing uses for wildlife products and new markets to promote the access to, and use of, wildlife as symbols of increasing wealth. With millions of disenfranchised communities living around, and often within, the parks that are supposed to protect our wildlife, poaching kingpins have no shortage of

OPPOSITE: The prehensile lip of a black rhinoceros. Photo: Bruno Zanzottera.

PREVIOUS SPREAD: Where rhino roam. Photo: Dana Allen.

desperate human beings willing to do their killing and thus kick-start a chain of wildlife trafficking that spans continents and societies.

It is into this murky underworld of not only the criminal actions, but also of the underlying human nature that drives them, that the rhino and their wildlife counterparts, such as lions, tigers, bears, elephants and pangolins, have found that their future has now plunged.

Confronting this murky underbelly of humanity forms just one aspect of the modern conservation crisis. On the opposite end of the scale, where the 'good guys' are found working on solutions, exists another crisis for humanity. One that is characterised by divisive ideologies, aggressive infighting, ego wars and conflicting agendas. The trouble with the issues faced by those working on this end of the scale is that there exists little to no common objective and no unified force. Instead, our conflicting ideologies, objectives and ambitions serve to divide us and divert attention away from the real enemy, which is in itself a lot more unified and cohesive in its intentions.

No clearer example of this exists in the debate around whether or not the legal trade in rhino horn is the panacea to the rhino poaching crisis. Pitting the individuals and entities that do not believe that a legal trade in rhino horn is currently the solution to this highly complex situation, against those who do or those who stand to benefit from the trade in rhino horn, against each other under the premise that the former group is 'anti-sustainable use' or an 'ill-informed animal rights group' has become one of the greatest stumbling blocks, I believe, to finding solutions to ensure that free living rhino survive. The argument has devolved to low levels with those who express a concern for legalising the trade within the context of rampant corruption, highly organised trading networks and insufficient protection for free living rhino, being accused of working alongside poachers to drive the rhino to extinction and pocketing 'millions' of dollars in funding to drive fancy cars. Despite this rhetoric, no evidence has yet been presented of any NGO that has allegedly benefitted from or been incentivised to drive rhino to extinction, and I have yet to hear of anyone from the NGO sector who has been alleged to be involved in any rhino poaching or illegal trade activities.

To the contrary, many NGOs have stepped in to fill the void created by radically slashed budgets in our provincial and national reserves, and have provided basic items such as: gloves and razor blades for tissue sampling; diesel and fuel to support more regular patrols; food, uniforms and radios to assist rangers in their day-to-day field work; high-tech support in the form of training and deploying sniffer and tracking dogs; and the provision of microchips, satellite phones, drones and handheld devices for improved data collection. The EWT alone has trained nearly 2 000 members of the police, SARS and the various provincial conservation and law enforcement agencies on various aspects of wildlife crime, environmental law and trafficking methodologies. Enormous amounts of funding have been spent on supporting the communities, who live on the borders of our parks, to become more resilient to the appeal of poaching as an income generator by the provision of alternative livelihoods, education and training, job creation and skills development.

In the years following South Africa's transition to a democratic government, shifting government priorities saw provincial conservation budgets being slashed, posts in conservation departments being left vacant or frozen and poor to no attention being paid to adequately training and resourcing those at the frontline of conservation. Political interference and union intervention in the running of some of the provincial agencies resulted in key skills being lost and insufficient knowledge remaining in those in leadership positions of how to deal with the impending crisis of wildlife poaching and trafficking. As a result, many provincial reserves were slowly eroded with fences being cut, roads not maintained, irregular patrols being carried out, poor to little implementation of management plans, and a focus on the 'bums in beds' component of the reserve instead of its contribution to biodiversity and endangered species conservation.

Essentially, South Africa was caught with its pants down when the rhino poaching crisis hit our shores: we had poorly managed, poorly resourced and poorly governed conservation departments and reserves; and, as a result, we failed to act swiftly, appropriately and with vigour. It is against this backdrop that the NGO movement, the private sector and civil society in general, had to step up and play a significant role in ramping up our defence against the onslaught of wildlife crime. Private wildlife owners, NGOs, corporate South Africa and civilians have all stepped up and become critical players in the race to save the rhino. For the most part, this has been done with enormous amounts of goodwill, collaboration and a desire to ensure that South African wildlife persists in a free and wild state. We are *all* partners in this struggle and we are *all* important. The divisive nature of the discourse in some sectors can therefore only suggest that not everyone envisages the same outcome for our wildlife and that the development of a collective vision is perhaps the first priority.

Further evidence of an urgent need for a new collective vision for wildlife in South Africa is the push by a small private-sector community, and some in government, towards the intensive farming and mass production of wildlife for body parts and with no demonstrable conservation benefit whatsoever. This, they counter, is simply an extension of the concept of 'sustainable use' which is being redefined as 'use that never ends', as opposed to a more valid interpretation of this term, which is to use natural resources in such a way that they contribute to the sustained ecological functioning of the ecosystem in which they are found. With no strict conditions set for the utilisation of wildlife resources, which would for example ensure that they are utilised only in such a way that they contribute to the ecological integrity and functioning of viable ecosystems, it is all too simple to equate them to cattle or sheep, feedlot them for mass production and sell off their body parts under the premise that this is sustainable use. I would argue that this is not what was envisioned in the Convention on Biological Diversity and in the South African Constitution.

The argument for mass producing wildlife resources in intensive breeding operations has been justified by some as a means to supply Asian markets, control prices and regulate trade flows, protect wild sources, displace demand and in some cases, even 'flood' markets to drive down demand. As none of these theories have been proven to stem the illicit flows of contraband, they are not sound enough reasons to enter into an age of 'wildlife production' with its own set of highly unfavourable consequences. For one, it is well documented that a trade in captive-bred wildlife parts does not displace the market for wild bred and caught counterparts – it often just creates a new market. For another, the flows of legally acquired wildlife products present severe challenges for already besieged law-enforcement authorities and a confused public, as product availability is all too often assumed to imply product legality, and checks and balances are not robust enough to prevent this confusion for the man on the street. Furthermore, in a highly corrupt society, and a world where organised-crime forces are not likely to simply drop a product due to the fact that there may now be a legal supply available, one cannot assume that traders, suppliers and consumers of the 'real, wild thing' will now simply stop their use.

An additional threat is the significant risk and damage to South Africa's reputation as a place of wild beauty, the 'wild' African experience and a tourism sector that has been built on stories of ground-breaking national park establishment, global conservation success and a sense of place. The advent of canned lion hunting has been a stain on South Africa's aspirations to present itself as a destination that offers a 'true' wildlife experience to a wider diversity of tourists or big-game hunters, than the small handful that seek to kill a captive lion for the joy of seeing it die.

All that the mass production of farmed wildlife products has demonstrated is that a parallel industry is created for those who desire to consume, shoot or trade in wildlife products. This cannot be what the drafters of the term 'sustainable utilisation' meant when they recognised that humanity's ability to derive a benefit from a resource would ensure its ecological survival. This is why, in recent times, the EWT has embarked on an effort to promote the use of the term 'sustainable conservation' in order to remind us that utilisation must support the continued conservation of that resource and not simply its continued use. It is our hope that if we return to the ideology that utilisation of our natural resources should benefit the greater good and the conservation of those ecosystems and habitats that support us all, we may again become unified in our outlook on humanity and our own pathway towards survival.

But herein lies the challenge. How do we achieve a unified conservation voice out of a set of ideologies and commercial objectives that differ so vastly and are in fact often at odds with one another? How do we begin to engage in dialogue that is constructive in its outcome and less divisive in its impact? These may be philosophical questions that fall outside the scope of conservationists and biologists, but for them the solutions are critical. We cannot afford to argue, attack, insult, manoeuvre, plot and scheme under the guise of having a common conservation objective, which is arguably not the case at worst and confusing at best, when the enemy is quite clear on its distinct objective, and is far more organised and efficient in its way of achieving it.

We are living in a world in which rampant crime, greed, the rights of the individual to wealth, health, consumption, ownership and power by far outweigh the rights of others, present or future, to equity, sustainability and, in some cases, to life. The proliferation of wildlife crime in recent decades extends to far more than rhino and elephant – it includes species such as cycads for the collector, reptiles for the pet trade, and a variety of species of animal and plants for medical and consumptive use that is far too extensive to list here. This is not new. What *has* however changed in recent years and is driving this pattern to crisis levels and tipping points for many species is the following: the integration of these commodities into transnational crime networks as highly tradeable products; the increase in consumer buying power; escalating corruption locally and globally; greater consumer access through social media and the 'dark web'; declining and inadequate support for conservation agencies; and the premise that the conservation of wild things in wild places is no longer a government priority. Underpinning this all is the mass commodification of wildlife for short-term gain and hence, I would suggest, this can never be the solution.

The rhino has been an icon of African wildlife for centuries and, in recent decades, it has become the icon of African conservation. I would now like to suggest that we escalate the rhino to the status of an icon for the future of humanity, as we face the truth about ourselves as a species that is able and willing to surrogate millennia of evolutionary biology and the aspirations of every wild and free species for the gains of artificial wealth, dubious health benefits, market control, power and ego. The fate of the rhino will become the fate of every other species that man determines has a value for consumers, traders, owners, buyers, thrill chasers and trophy seekers.

The rhino does not belong to us. It belongs to no one. All that we own is the responsibility of ensuring that it persists and that future books on the rhino are written about its expanded range and not its declining future.

John Hanks

Clive Walker has a deserved reputation for being one of Africa's conservation champions, a prolific writer, talented wildlife artist, and one of those rare public speakers who never fails to captivate audiences of all age groups with his passion and enthusiasm, as I have witnessed on many occasions. In writing *Rhino Revolution* he has teamed up with his son Anton to address a highly controversial question that unfortunately is polarising environmental NGOs and their donors, namely what should be done to secure a sustainable future for the five species of rhinos?

I have no doubt that many people will be looking forward to what they have to say, and I was most encouraged to read the clear and unambiguous arguments they have presented in favour of a legal trade in rhino horn, which I need not repeat here. Too many opposing this option bring nothing new to the debate. A regurgitation of their ossified proposals, which have clearly failed, is regrettably often accompanied by a shrillness and stridency from those who are the least willing to compromise, understandably sowing confusion in the minds of donors who genuinely want to help but are looking for guidance on what to do.

The donor's dilemma on which rhino project to support is exacerbated by the vagueness of some of the appeals, and an unacceptable paucity of information on the results of the funding of these appeals to 'save the rhino'. The more reputable NGOs listed by the Walkers are far more circumspect in their articulation of needs and priorities for rhino conservation, recognising that there is no one 'silver bullet' to halt poaching, and presenting regular audited financial statements and progress reports on what has been achieved. What is long overdue is a careful and thorough investigation of the results of how the millions of dollars for rhinos raised by the dubious practitioners have been spent.

We should not be surprised that the often brutal killing of charismatic species such as elephants and rhinos attracts a disproportionate amount of attention and resources.[1] I have used the word 'disproportionate' for the very good reason that this fixation on a very small number of species diverts funding from what I believe should be much higher priorities, many of which are directly and indirectly strongly influenced by the high rates of human population growth and its environmental and social impacts, linked to increasing poverty, declining food security, and unemployment. The latest population projections from the United Nations Population Division include the very worrying prediction that more than half of the expected global population growth between now and 2100 will occur in Africa, with the present population of 1.26 billion estimated to increase to 4.47 billion by the end of this century.[2] Today, 41% of the African population is under the age of 15. Rapid population growth is typically associated with a large number of poorly educated young men with few job opportunities, a recipe for violence, conflict, and an increasing number turning to wildlife crime.

The concentration of population growth in the poorest countries will make it harder for those governments to eradicate poverty and allocate funds for environmental conservation activities, and top of my list of concerns must be the unprecedented threats to Africa's designated Protected Areas (PAs). These should be the crown jewels of the global commitment to biodiversity conservation – vital areas where natural evolutionary and ecological processes can operate with minimal human disturbance – yet they are becoming increasingly isolated from one another, exacerbated by accelerating land transformation in surrounding areas and an increase in people living in poverty and facing food insecurity. The PAs themselves are directly threatened by human encroachment, hunting for bush-meat and by the illegal wildlife trade.

Major shortfalls in financial support for virtually every PA in Africa is impacting on the number and quality of staff, the development and maintenance of roads, buildings, vehicles and fences, and a serious decline in research activities and basic monitoring.[3] Furthermore, there is a continued alienation of adjacent rural communities by punitive measures to protect wildlife, which in too many cases make little or no attempt to help these people develop alternative sustainable livelihoods, a real concern that the Walkers have clearly enunciated. Unless local people and their national governments want to conserve wildlife, it will not survive.

I would also like to see much more recognition and support being given in addition to this book to the major contributions that are being made to biodiversity conservation in some of the areas outside of the PAs, such as the private land owners (particularly in South Africa), and the communal areas (as demonstrated with the Conservancies in Namibia). Today over 6 500 rhino are found on private reserves in South Africa, 37% of the national herd and more than the rest of Africa combined. John Hume – the world's largest private rhino owner with 1 533 on his 8 000-hectare ranch – has successfully bred over 1 000 rhinos on his property, and he is the first to appreciate that he has a massive responsibility for the future to help with restocking the PAs that have lost all their animals. He has done this with no help from government and the NGO community. Sadly, he is unjustifiably branded as a greedy land-owner, and does not get the credit and recognition he deserves.

Linked to the private-sector initiatives is the general lack of awareness of the vital importance of developing a sustainable wildlife economy. The misguided but well-meaning campaigns to eliminate consumptive use of wildlife ignore the realities of poverty in Africa, the extent, impact and costs of mitigating intensifying human–wildlife conflict, and the underfunding of protected areas. Rhino poaching should be viewed as an economic problem. With ongoing consumer demand driving up prices for rhino horn, incentives for illegal activity increase relative to the incentives to protect live rhinos. Where wild rhino populations have survived, this has been due to adequate enforcement spending and rhino-related economic benefit flows to relevant local people, not necessarily because of restrictions on rhino horn trade.[4] It was the late internationally renowned and highly respected rhino conservationist Ian Player who more than 50 years ago identified the positive role the private sector and private reserves could play in the conservation of the species, through range expansion and sustainable utilisation by hunting. He said: 'To exist in an unnatural world, animals must have a commercial value that can be exploited. Without it, their chances of survival are slim.'

I was delighted to see that the book has also been dedicated to the field staff who have the demanding and increasingly dangerous task of protecting what the authors have called the 'unsung heroes in this battle to keep rhinos alive'. Throughout the continent, the majority of conservation staff do not receive adequate remuneration for the life-threatening situations they face in combatting wildlife crime, and this must change.

The Walkers would be the first to recognise the urgent need to promote a far greater awareness that environmental conservation is far more than the 'charismatic megafauna', but instead a vitally important prerequisite for building a sustainable future for the whole of Africa, with a renewed emphasis to conserve the full spectrum of biodiversity, a message actively promoted today at the Lapalala Wilderness School, which Clive Walker founded over 30 years ago. Recent surveys have documented disturbing population declines and even local extinctions of select pollinator species. For example, bees pollinate human food worldwide valued at more than US$350 billion,[5] and food security is already being severely compromised by decimation of populations of these and other pollinators.

Of course, rhinos need all the support they can get in this last stand, as Clive and Anton have portrayed with adroitness and passion, but so do thousands of other species and the ecosystems in which they live. Perhaps new words are needed in the soup of the rhino conservation vocabulary, not just for the sake of novelty, but to stimulate and encourage the often jaded palate of the general public to embrace rhinos not just as charismatic species in their own right, but as *environmental conservation ambassadors*, inspiring awareness of nature's extraordinary celebration of biodiversity, and hopefully bringing together a divided conservation paradigm into a united and harmonious ensemble.

FOLLOWING SPREAD: A breathtaking view of the famed Okavango Delta, home once again to both species of African rhino. Photo: Wilderness Safaris/Dana Allen.

Endnotes, Bibliography,
About the Authors &
Acknowledgements

Endnotes

Chapter 1
1. The African Rhino Specialist Group (AfRSG), 2016.
2. www.savetherhino.org/rhino_info/poaching_statistics.

Chapter 2
1. Offord-Woolley, S. 2016. 'China and Vietnam heavily involved in global rhino horn trade'. Available at: www.savetherhino.org/latest_news/news/1499_china_vietnam_heavily_involved_in_global_rhino_horn_trade (accessed on 2 November 2017).
2. Savides, M. 2016. 'Activists take the fight for the rhino to the courts – the new front-line'. *Sunday Times*.
3. Hanks, Dr J. 2016. *Rhino Files*. Private Rhino Owner's Association. For more information visit www.rhinoalive.com.
4. Vaughan, A. 2012. 'Affluent Vietnamese driving rhino horn poaching in South Africa, report warns'. *The Guardian*. Available at: www.theguardian.com/environment/2012/jul/23/vietnam-rhino-horn-poaching-south-africa (accessed on 2 November 2017).
5. Vaughan, A. 2012.
6. Reprobate. 2013. 'The People of South Africa: Chinese South Africans'. *Reprobate*. Available at: https://reprobate.co.za/the-people-of-south-africa-chinese-south-africans (accessed on 2 November 2017).
7. Darlington, M. 2010. 'Top 20 countries with most endangered species'. *Mother Nature Network*. Available at: www.mnn.com/earth-matters/animals/stories/infographic-top-20-countries-with-most-endangered-species (accessed on 2 November 2017).
8. More information on the Père David's deer is available at: https://en.wikipedia.org/wiki/P%C3%A8re_David%27s_deer (accessed on 2 November 2017).
9. More information on the rhinoceroses of China is available at: https://en.wikipedia.org/wiki/Rhinoceroses_in_ancient_China (accessed on 2 November 2017).
10. Mitchley, A & Sapa. 2015. '1215 rhino poached, aluta continua'. *The Citizen*. Available at: https://citizen.co.za/news/south-africa/312380/rhino-poaching-increased-2014/ (accessed 2 November 2017). The Department of Environmental Affairs, for reasons unknown, has since stopped releasing regular data on rhino deaths or arrests.
11. Savides, M. 2016. 'Activists take the fight for the rhino to the courts – the new front-line'. *Sunday Times*.
12. Save the Rhino. 2017. 'Poaching Statistics'. Available at: www.savetherhino.org/rhino_info/poaching_statistics (accessed on 2 November 2017).
13. Savides, M. 2016. 'Activists take the fight for the rhino to the courts – the new frontline'. *Sunday Times*, 25 September.
14. Fenio, K.G. 2014. 'Poaching Rhino Horn in South Africa and Mozambique: Community and Expert Views from the Trenches'. US Department of State.
15. savetherhino.org. 2016. 'Corruption at the highest level'. Available at: www.savetherhino.org/latest_news/news/1521_corruption_at_highest_levels (accessed on 14 November 2017).
16. Ngubane, S. 2016. 'ANC is recycling corruption, says Buthelezi'. Available at: https://www.iol.co.za/news/politics/anc-is-recycling-corruption-says-buthelezi-2033903 (accessed on 2 November 2017).
17. Pityana, Sipho, Anglogold Ashanti Chairman, speech at 2016 Mining Indaba, Johannesburg, 5 October 2016, reports in *The Star*, 9 November 2016.

18. Offord-Woolley, S. 2016. 'China and Vietnam heavily involved in global rhino horn trade'. Available at: www.savetherhino.org/latest_news/news/1499_china_vietnam_heavily_involved_in_global_rhino_horn_trade (accessed on 2 November 2017).

19. Oxpeckers Reporters. 2015. 'Caught in the crossfire: how cattle and Chinese mining interests are killing off Namibia's black rhinos'. Available at: https://oxpeckers.org/2015/07/caught-in-the-crossfire-how-cattle-and-chinese-mining-interests-are-killing-off-namibias-black-rhinos/ (accessed on 2 November 2017).

20. Report by Minister of Water and Environmental Affairs, Edna Molewa. Visit www.environment.gov.za for more information.

21. DEA press release. 1 November 2015. Available at: www.environment.gov.za.

22. Herman, P. 2016. 'To save rhino, we need to save the poor – SANParks scientist'. Available at: http://www.news24.com/SouthAfrica/News/to-save-rhino-we-need-to-save-the-poor-sanparks-scientist-20160914 (accessed on 2 November 2017).

23. Knight, M. 2016. 'Calling all rhino owners'. *Wildlife Ranching*. Available at: https://www.rhinoalive.com/wp-content/uploads/2016/06/RS_Mike-Knight-DPS.pdf (accessed on 2 November 2017).

24. Joubert, P. 2015. 'R440m spent but rhinos still slaughtered'. Available at: http://city-press.news24.com/News/R440m-spent-but-rhinos-still-slaughtered-20150630 (accessed on 2 November 2017).

25. Christy, B. 2016. 'Deadly Trade'. *National Geographic*, October, p 56.

26. Motylska, I. 2015. 'Going, going, gone: Saving Africa's rhino's extinction'. Available at: http://venturesafrica.com/features/going-going-gone-saving-africas-rhinos-from-extinction/ (accessed 2 November 2017).

27. Walker, C. 2012. Presentation given to the Private Rhino Owners Association Parliamentary Portfolio Committee, chaired by Dr Mike Knight. Onderstepoort, 26 January.

28. Jones, Pelham, chair, Private Rhino Owners Association Journal, first edition, overview of South African privately-owned reserves with rhino populations, February 2016. Visit www.rhinoalive.com for more information.

29. Newsweek. 1993. 'Killing the Trade in Rhino Horn', *Newsweek* (Asian, European, African/Middle Eastern and Latin American editions), CXXI (25), 21 June 1993, 48–52.

30. Martin, E.B & Vigne, L. 2016. 'High rhino horn price's drive poaching'. *SWARA*, 40(3): 42–46.

31. Anderson, Peter. Personal communication. 2016.

32. Offord-Woolley, S. 2017. 'We need to celebrate our success and stay positive for the task ahead'. Available at: www.savetherhino.org/latest_news/blog/celebrating_success (accessed on 6 November 2017).

33. www.savetherhino.org.

Chapter 3

1. Carnie, T. 2017. 'Poaching surge rocks flagship KZN reserve'. *The Sunday Times*. 14 May.

2. Saayman, M. & Saayman, A. 2016. 'Is the Rhino worth saving? A sustainable perspective'. Wildlife Ranching, 4, DOI: http://dx.doi.org/10.1080/09669582.2016.1197229.

3. www.statsas.gov.za/publications/report-03-51-02/Report-03-51-022015.

4. Saayman, M. & Saayman, A. 2016. 'Is the Rhino worth saving? A sustainable perspective'. Wildlife Ranching, 4, DOI: http://dx.doi.org/10.1080/09669582.2016.1197229.

5. Hitchens, Peter, personal notes on the chronological history of Imfolozi Game Reserve 1818–1962, unpublished.
6. Hitchins, P., 'The black rhinoceros in South Africa', EWT newsletter, 2, 1975.
7. Flamand, Dr J. Personal communication. Rhino Range Expansion Programme, WWF. 2016.
8. WWF, Black Rhino Range Expansion Project fact file, undated.
9. Wilderness Safaris. Newsletters and personal communication. Chris Roche. 2016.
10. Smith, J-M. 2017. 'Elephant poaching up, rhino down (Namibia)'. Originally published in the *Namibian Sun*. 13 January. Available at: www.conservationaction.co.za/recent-news/elephant-rhino-poaching-namibia (accessed 5 October 2017).
11. www.isimangaliso.com.

Chapter 4

1. www.rhinoresourcecenter.com
2. Martin, E.B., *Rhino Exploitation: The Trade in Rhino Products in India, Indonesia, Malaysia, Burma, Japan, & S. Korea*, Hong Kong, WWF, 1983
3. Humane Society International. Undated. 'Rhinoceros horn stockpiles – a serious threat to rhinos'.
4. Talbot, L. 1983. Preface to Martin, E.B. *Rhino Exploitation: The Trade in Rhino Products in India, Indonesia, Malaysia, Burma, Japan and South Korea*, Hong Kong, World Wildlife Fund.
5. Martin, E.B. 1983. *Rhino Exploitation: The Trade in Rhino Products in India, Indonesia, Malaysia, Burma, Japan and South Korea, Hong Kong*. World Wildlife Fund.
6. Leader-Williams, N. & Albon, SD. 1988. 'Allocation of Resources for Conservation', *Nature* 336.
7. Personal communication from T. Conway, manager of iSimangaliso Wetland Park, KwaZulu-Natal, July 2015/2016.
8. Personal communication from Michelle Pfab, South African Biodiversity Institute, 2 September 2016.
9. Olver, C. 2010. 'Can't park a problem', *Sunday Times*, 25 November.
10. Emslie, R. & Brooks, M. 1999. African Rhino: Status Survey and Conservation Action Plan. IUCN/SSC African Rhino Specialist Group, IUCN, Gland, Switzerland and Cambridge, UK.
11. Reference needed for Glenn Phillips quote.
12. Pelham Jones. Personal communication. 2016.
13. United Nations, Department of Economic and Social Affairs, Population Division. 2017. World Population Prospects: The 2017 Revision, Key Findings and Advance Tables. Working Paper No. ESA/P/WP/248.
14. Personal communication from Pelham Jones, 2017.
15. Visit www.rhinoalive.com for more information.
16. Jones, P. 2011. *Rhino Files*. Private Rhino Owner's Association. For more information visit www.rhinoalive.com.
17. SA News. 2015. 'South Africa's relationship with China – by the numbers'. Available at: https://businesstech.co.za/news/government/99786/south-africas-relationship-with-china-by-the-numbers/ (accessed on 6 November 2017).
18. Knight, M. 2016. *Rhino Files*. Private Rhino Owner's Association. For more information visit www.rhinoalive.com.
19. Emslie, R & Brooks, M. 1999. African Rhino: Status Survey and Conservation Action

Plan, IUCN/SSC African Rhino Specialist Group, IUCN, Gland, Switzerland and Cambridge, UK.

20. Hughes, G, quoted in Walker, C. & Walker, A. 2012. *The Rhino Keepers*. Johannesburg: Jacana Media.

21. Buys, D. 1997. 'Rhino Watch', *Rhino and Elephant Foundation Journal*, 6 July.

22. Eugene Lapointe, former CITES secretary-general, remarks at CoP17, Johannesburg, 2016.

23. Swanepoel, G., 'The illegal trade in rhino horn as an example of an endangered species', paper presented at the Third International Criminological Congress hosted by IDASA and CRIMSA at UNISA, South Africa, 1996.

24. Dr Michael Knight and Dr Richard Emslie from the African Rhino Specialist Group, quoted in Walker, C. & Walker, A. 2012. *Rhino Keepers*. Johannesburg: Jacana Media.

25. Personal communication from John Hanks, October 2016.

26. Michael Eustace, quoted in Walker, C. & Walker, A. 2012. *The Rhino Keepers*. Johannesburg: Jacana Media.

27. Personal communication, John Hanks, October 2016.

28. Hanks, J. 2015. *Operation Lock and the War on Rhino Poaching*. Cape Town: Penguin Books; and from the IUCN website: www.iucn.org.

Chapter 5

1. Letter from Dr Anthony Hall-Martin to DSWF, 18 February 2012.

2. 'Focus on black rhino (*Diceros bicornis bicornis*) population dynamics and a formula for successful conservation of the species 2002–2012', published in the proceedings of the 2013 International Elephant & Rhino Conservation & Research Symposium.

3. Reproductive indicators, parameters defined by Raoul du Toit. Guidelines for implementing SADC Rhino Conservation Strategies, 2006.

4. The 2013 International Elephant & Rhino Conservation & Research Symposium was held in Pittsburgh, USA.

Chapter 6

1. Abridged from an article by Jim Feely, first published in 2007 in *Pachyderm Journal of the Africa*, 43:111–15.

2. Barrow J. 1801. *An account of Travels into Southern Africa*, vol. 1, London: T. Cadell & W. Davies, p. 395, map.

3. Skead CJ. 1980. *Historical Mammal Incidence in the Cape Province, vol. 1, The western and northern Cape*. Cape Town: Department of Nature and Environmental Conservation, pp. 290, 298.

4. Bradlow E and Bradlow F, eds. 1979. William Somerville's narrative of his journeys to the Eastern Cape Frontier and to Lattakoe 1799–1802, appendix 1, pp 205–235; P. Borcherds's letter to his father, Van Riebeeck Society (2nd series, no. 10), Cape Town, unpublished original in Dutch.

5. Theal GM. 1899. Records of the Cape Colony, vol. 4, From May 1801 to February 1803, Report by P.J. Truter and W. Somerville to the governor at the Cape. Government Cape Colony, London.

6. Bradlow, E & Bradlow, F, eds. 1979. William Somerville's narrative of his journeys to the Eastern Cape Frontier and to Lattakoe 1799–1802, appendix 1, pp 205–235; P. Borcherds's letter to his father, Van Riebeeck Society (2nd series, no. 10), Cape Town, p. 219.

7. Harris WC. 1986. Portraits of the game and wild animals of southern Africa: delineated

from life in their native haunts. Alberton: Galago Press (both rhino plates first published 1841), p. 74.

8. Tulloch S, ed. 1993. *Reader's Digest Oxford complete wordfinder*. London: Reader's Digest, pp 359–436.

9. Tulloch S, ed. 1993. *Reader's Digest Oxford complete wordfinder*. London: Reader's Digest, pp 359–436; Eksteen LC, ed. 1997. *Major Dictionary: Afrikaans-English, English-Afrikaans*, 14th ed. Cape Town: Pharos.

Chapter 7

1. All information on the five living rhino species that appears in this section was obtained from the International Rhino Foundation website. Visit http://rhinos.org to access this information.

2. lonerhino.org/rhino.

3. African/Asian Rhino Specialist Group, 2016. Available at: http://rhinos.org/species/white-rhino/ (accessed on 6 October 2017).

4. African/Asian Rhino Specialist Group, 2016. Available at: http://rhinos.org/species/black-rhino/ (accessed on 6 October 2017).

5. Kiwia, H.D. 1989. 'Ranging patterns of the black rhinoceros (Diceros bicornis (L.)) in Ngorongoro Crater, Tanzania'. *African Journal of Ecology*, 27: 305–312. Available at: http://www.rhinoresourcecenter.com/index.php?act=refs&CODE=ref_detail&id=1165237477 (accessed on 6 October 2017).

6. Feely, J. 2002. 'Black or white? The identification and significance of rhinoceroses in South African Bushman rock art'. *The Digging Stick*, Vol. 19(2): 9–12.

7. International Rhino Foundation. http://rhinos.org/species/sumatran-rhino/ (accessed on 6 October 2017).

8. International Rhino Foundation. http://rhinos.org/species/sumatran-rhino/ (accessed on 6 October 2017).

9. International Rhino Foundation. http://rhinos.org/species/javan-rhino/ (accessed on 6 October 2017).

10. International Rhino Foundation. http://rhinos.org/species/greater-one-horned-rhino/ (accessed on 6 October 2017).

Afterwords

1. Krause, M. & Robinson, K. 2017. Charismatic Species and Beyond: How Cultural Schemas and Organisational Routines Shape Conservation. *Conservation and Society* 15(3): 71–79.

2. United Nations, Department of Economic and Social Affairs, Population Division. 2017. World Population Prospects: The 2017 Revision, Key Findings and Advance Tables. Working Paper No. ESA/P/WP/248.

3. Watson, JEM, Dudley, N, Segan, DB & Hockings, M. 2014. 'The performance and potential of protected areas'. *Nature* 515: 67–73.

4. t' Sas-Rolfes, M. 2016. 'Rhino Poaching: What is the Solution?' *The Solutions Journal* 7(1): 38–45. Available at: www.thesolutionsjournal.com/article/rhino-poaching-what-is-the-solution/ (accessed on 3 November 2017).

5. Weyler, R. 2013. 'Worldwide honey bee collapse: A lesson in ecology'. Available at: www.resilience.org/stories/2013-06-12/worldwide-honey-bee-collapse-a-lesson-in-ecology/ (accessed on 3 November 2017).

Bibliography

African/Asian Rhino Specialist Group/TRAFFIC, 2016.

Alexander J.E., *An expedition of discovery into the interior of Africa, through the hitherto undescribed countries of the great Namaquas, Boschmans and Hill Damaras,* vol. 1, Henry Colburn, London, 1838.

Andersson C.J., *The Okavango River: a narrative of travel, exploration and adventure,* Hurst and Blackett, London, 1861.

Andersson, J.G. 1934. *Children of the Yellow Earth: Studies in Prehistoric China.* London: Kegan Paul, Trench, Trübner & Co.

Astley-Maberley C.T., *The game animals of southern Africa,* Nelson, Johannesburg, 1963.

Baines T., *Explorations in south-west Africa,* Longmans, Green, London, 1864.

Baldwin, W. C. 1967 (first published in 1894). *African Hunting and Adventure.* Cape Town: Struik Publishers.

Barrow J. 1801. *An account of travels into southern Africa,* vol. 1, T. Cadell & W. Davies, London.

Bauer, W. 1976. *China and the Search for Happiness: Recurring Themes in Four Thousand Years of Chinese Cultural History.* New York: Seabury Press.

Bradlow E. and Bradlow F., eds. 1979. *William Somerville's narrative of his journeys to the Eastern Cape Frontier and to Lattakoe 1799–1802,* Cape Town: Van Riebeeck Society, 2nd series, no. 10, pp. 1–204.

Brander, M. 1988. *The Big Game Hunters.* London: The Sportsman's Press.

But, P., Lung, L. & Tam, K. 1991. 'Ethnopharmacology of rhinoceros horn II: antipyretic effects of prescriptions containing rhinoceros horn or water buffalo horn'. *Journal of Ethnopharmacology,* 33: 45–50.

Chang, K. 1980. *Shang Civilization.* New Haven: Yale University Press.

Chauvet, J.M. 1996. *Chauvet Cave: The Discovery of the World's Oldest Paintings.* London: Thames & Hudson.

Cumming R.G. 1850. *Five Years of a Hunter's Life,* London: John Murray.

Dala-Clayton, B. & Child, B. 2003. 'Lessons from Luangwa'. International Institute for Environment & Development, *Wildlife and Development Series,* 13.

Darwin, C. 1859. *On the Origin of Species.* London: John Murray.

De Alessi, M. 2000. 'Private conservation and black rhinos in Zimbabwe: Savé Valley and Bubiana Conservancies'. Harare: Centre for Private Conservation (private conservation case study).

De Watteville, V. 1935. *Speak to the Earth.* London: Methuen & Co.

Doke, C.M. & Vilakazi, B.W. 1953. *Zulu-English dictionary,* 2nd rev. ed., Johannesburg: Witwatersrand University Press.

Du Toit, J. 1993. 'It's a matter of principle'. *Saturday Star,* 11 September.

Du Toit R. 2006. *Guidelines for implementing SADC Rhino Conservation Strategies.* SADC Regional Programme for Rhino Conservation: Zimbabwe.

Dubs, H. 1955. *The History of the Former Han Dynasty, by Ban Gu.* Baltimore: Waverly Press.

Edwards, M. 2000. 'Indus: clues to an ancient civilization'. *National Geographic,* 197(6):108–131.

Eksteen, L.C., ed. 1997. *Major Dictionary: Afrikaans-English, English-Afrikaans*, 14th ed., Pharos, Cape Town.

Ellis, B. 1994. 'Game conservation in Zululand 1824–1947; changing perspectives'. *Natalia*, 23/24: 27–44.

Emslie, R. & Brooks, M. 1999. 'African Rhino, Status Survey and Conservation Plan'. Gland, Switzerland: IUCN SSC African Rhino Specialist Group.

Emslie, R.H. and Adcock, K. 2013. '*Diceros bicornis* Black Rhinoceros (Browse Rhinoceros, Hook-Lipped Rhinoceros)' in Kingdom J. and Hoffmann, M. (eds), *Mammals of Africa, Volume V, Carnivores, Pangolins, Equids and Rhinoceros*. Bloomsbury Publishing: 455–466.

Enright, K. 2008. *Rhinoceros*. London: Reakton Books.

Feely, J. 2002. 'Black or white? The identification and significance of rhinoceroses in South African Bushman rock art'. *The Digging Stick*, 19(2): 9–12.

Feely, J. 2007. 'Black rhino, white rhino – what's in a name?' *Pachyderm Journal of the Africa*, 43: 111–15.

Gerstaecker, F. 1853. 'Rhinoceros hunting in Java'. *Reynolds's Miscellany of Romance, General Literature, Science, and Art*, 10: 277.

Groves, C.P. & Leslie, D. M. 2011. '*Rhinoceros sondaicus*'. American Society of Mammalogists, *Mammalian Species*, 43: 190–208.

Gurung, K.K. 1983. *Heart of the Jungle*. London: Andre Deutsch.

Hall-Martin, A., Walker, C. & Bothma, J du P. 1988. *Kaokoveld: The Last Wilderness*. Johannesburg: Southern Books.

Harris W.C. 1986 (both rhino plates first published 1841). *Portraits of the game and wild animals of southern Africa: delineated from life in their native haunts*, Alberton: Galago Press.

Hearn, B. 1999. *White Hunters: The Golden Age of African Safaris*, New York: Henry Holt and Co, Inc.

Hieronymus, T.L. & Witmer, L.M. 2004. 'Rhinoceros horn attachment: anatomy and histology of a dermally influenced bone rugosity'. *Journal of Morphology*, 260(3): 298.

Hitchins, P. 1975. 'The black rhinoceros in South Africa'. *EWT Newsletter*, 2.

Hitchins, P. 2002. 'Historical notes on the Khama Rhino Sanctuary, Botswana'. Unpublished.

Hunter, J.A. 1952. *Hunter*. London: Hamish Hamilton.

Laurie, W.A. 1978. 'The ecology and behaviour of the greater one horned rhinoceros'. PhD thesis, Selwyn College, University of Cambridge.

Leader-Williams, N. 1992. 'The world trade in rhino horn: A Review'. A TRAFFIC Network Report.

Leader-Williams, N. & Albon, S.D. 1988. 'Allocation of resources for conservation'. *Nature*, 336.

Lefeuvre, J. 1990. 'Rhinoceros and wild buffaloes north of the Yellow River at the end of the Shang Dynasty. *MonumentaSericaJournal*, 39: 131–157.

Maguire, J. 1998. *Makapansgat: A guide to the paleontological and archaeological sites of the Makapansgat Valley*. Pretoria: Transvaal Museum.

Marina, C. 1991. *Kenya: World Travel Guide*. London: Bartholomew.

Marnham, Patrick. 1980. *Fantastic Invasions: Notes on contemporary Africa*. New York: Harcourt Brace Jovanovich.

Martin, E.B. & Martin, C. B. 1982. *Run Rhino Run*. London: Chatto & Windus.

Martin, E.B. & Vigne, L. 1992. 'Zimbabwe's rhinos under threat'. *SWARA*, 15.

Martin, E.B. 1983. *Rhino Exploitation. The Trade in Rhino Products in India, Indonesia, Malaysia, Burma, Japan & South Korea.* Hong Kong: WWF.

Milledge, S. 2007. 'Rhino-related crimes in Africa: an overview of poaching, seizure and stockpile data for the period 2000–2005'. CoP14 Information Document: CoP14 Inf. 41, CITES Secretariat, The Hague.

Mini, B.M., Tshabe, S.L., Shoba F.M. & Van der Westhuizen P.N. 2003. *The Greater Dictionary of isiXhosa*, vol. 2. K-P. Alice: IsiXhosa National Lexicography Unit, University of Fort Hare.

Mossop, E.E. 1947. *Lives of the Earlier Krugers Told by a Revised Genealogical Table.* Archives Yearbook for South African History, Government Printer, Cape Town.

Olver, C. 2010. 'Can't park a problem'. *Sunday Times.* 25 November.

Owen T.R.H. 1956. 'The black and white rhinoceros'. *Uganda Wild Life and Sport* 1:27–31, Uganda Game & Fisheries Department, Entebbe.

Pitman C.R.S. 1931b. *A Game Warden among his Charges*, London: Nisbet & Co.

Pitman C.R.S. 1931a. 'Hobnobbing with the white rhinoceros', *Asia* 31:446–451, quoted in Rookmaaker, 2003.

Pitman, D. 1991. *Rhinos: Past, Present and Future?* Harare: Roblaw Publishers.

Player I.C. 1972. *The White Rhino Saga.* London: Collins.

Prothero, D.R. 1991. 'Fifty million years of rhinoceros evolution'. In Ryder, O. A. (ed) *Proceedings of the International Rhino Conference*, San Diego: San Diego Zoological Society.

Rackham, O. 2001 (first published in 1990). *Trees and Woodlands in the British Landscape: The complete history of Britain's trees, woods and hedgerows*, London: Phoenix Press.

Roberts, A. 1951. *The Mammals of South Africa.* Johannesburg: Trustees of the Mammals of South Africa Book Fund.

Rookmaaker, L.C. 2003. 'Why the name of the white rhinoceros is not appropriate'. *Pachyderm*, 34: 88–93.

Rookmaaker, L.C. 1981. 'Early rhinoceros systematics'. *Papers from the Conference to Celebrate the Centenary of the British Museum (Natural History).* London: Society for the Bibliography of Natural History.

Ryder, M.L. 1962. 'Structure of rhinoceros horn'. *Nature*, 193 (4821): 1119–1201.

Saayman, M. & Saayman, A. 2016. 'Is the Rhino worth saving? A sustainable perspective'. *Wildlife Ranching*, vol 4, DOI: http://dx.doi.org/10.1080/09669582.2016.1197229.

Savides, M. 2016. 'Activists take the fight for the rhino to the courts – the new frontline'. *Sunday Times.*

Selous, F.C. 1881. *A Hunter's Wanderings in Africa.* London: Macmillan.

Selous F.C. 1908. *African Nature Notes and Reminiscences.* London: Macmillan.

Shortridge, G.C. 1934. *The Mammals of South West Africa*, vol. 1. London: William Heinemann.

Skead, C.J. 1987. *Historical Mammal Incidence in the Cape Province*, vol. 2: *The Eastern Half of the Cape Province, including Ciskei, Transkei and East Griqualand.* Cape Town. Department of Nature and Environmental Conservation.

Skead, C.J. 1980. *Historical Mammal Incidence in the Cape Province*, vol. 1: *The western and northern Cape.* Cape Town: Department of Nature and Environmental Conservation.

Skinner, J.D. & Chimimba, C.T. 2005. *Mammals of the Southern African Sub-region*, 3rd ed., Pretoria: Pretoria University.

Skinner, J.D & Smithers, R.H.N. 1990. *Mammals of the Southern African Sub-region*, 2nd ed. Pretoria: Pretoria University.

Smith, J-M. 2017. 'Elephant poaching up, rhino down (Namibia)'. Available at: www.conservationaction.co.za/recent-news/elephant-rhino-poaching-namibia (accessed 5 October 2017).

Smithers, R.H.N. 1983. *Mammals of the southern African Sub-region*. Pretoria: Pretoria University.

Smithers, R. & Skinner, J.D. 1990. *Mammals of the Southern African Sub-region*. Pretoria: University of Pretoria.

Soame, J. 1957. 'The Chinese rhinoceros and Chinese carvings in rhinoceros horn'. *Transactions of the Oriental Ceramic Society 1954–1955*, 29.

Steedman, A. 1835. *Wanderings and Adventure in the Interior of southern Africa*, vol 1. London: Collins.

Swanepoel, G. 1996. 'The illegal trade in rhino horn as an example of an endangered species'. Paper presented at the Third International Criminological Congress hosted by IDASA and CRIMSA at UNISA, South Africa.

Theal, G.M. 1899. *Records of the Cape Colony*, vol. 4, *From May 1801 to February 1803*, Report by P.J. Truter and W. Somerville to the governor at the Cape. Government Cape Colony, London, 1899.

Tiley, S. 2004. *Mapungubwe*. Cape Town: Sunbird Publishing.

Tulloch S., ed. 1993. *Reader's Digest Oxford Complete Wordfinder*, Reader's Digest, London: 359–436.

Van Strien, N.J. 1986. 'The Sumatran rhinoceros, *Dicerorhinus sumatrensis*, in the Gunung Leuser National Park, Sumatra, Indonesia: its distribution, ecology and conservation'. Mammalia Depicta, 12.

Van Strien, N.J. 2005. 'Javanrhinoceros'. Save the Rhinos: EAZA Rhino Campaign 2005/6 info pack. London: Save the Rhinos.

Van Strien, N.J. 2005. 'Sumatran rhinoceros'. Save the Rhinos: EAZA Rhino Campaign 2005/6 info pack. London: Save the Rhinos.

Vaughn, A. 2012. 'Affluent Vietnamese driving rhino horn poaching in South Africa, report warns.' *The Guardian*. Available at: https://www.theguardian.com/environment/2012/jul/23/vietnam-rhino-horn-poaching-south-africa.

Walker, C. & Potgieter, H. 1989. *Okavango from the Air*. Cape Town: Struik Publishers.

Walker, C. & Walker, A. 2012. *The Rhino Keepers*. Johannesburg: Jacana Media.

Walker, C. 1992. 'Botswana aerial census'. *Rhino & Elephant Journal*, 7.

Walker, C. 1996. *Signs of the Wild*. Cape Town: Struik Publishers.

Walker, C. 2013. *Baobab Trails*. Johannesburg: Jacana Media.

Walker, C. 2016. *Signs of the Wild*. Cape Town: Struik New Holland.

Yanyan, D. & Qian, J. 2008. 'Proposal on protecting and sustainable use of rhinoceros' [in Chinese]. *Institute of Scientific & Technical Information of China, Resource Development & Market*, 24. In 'Wrathful Rhino'. *You*, 6 October 1988.

Zhufan, X. & Xiaokai, H., eds. 1984. *Dictionary of Traditional Chinese Medicine*. Hong Kong: The Commercial Press.

About the authors

Clive Walker entered the battle for the rhino with the founding of the Endangered Wildlife Trust in 1973. He co-founded the Rhino and Elephant Foundation and the African Rhino Owners Association, and served on the IUCN African Rhino Specialist Group for close on 14 years. He served as a member of the South African Parks Board from 2000 to 2006.

Anton Walker, Clive's son, grew up largely at Lapalala Wilderness, the reserve that was to become an important rhino sanctuary and a world-class environmental school in the bush. Anton joined the permanent staff of the reserve in 1996 and was the general manager of the 45 000-hectare sanctuary until October 2017. He has since taken up the position of director and curator of the Waterberg Living Museum in the Waterberg of Limpopo. His knowledge of both species of rhino is extensive in all areas of management, capture, monitoring, field operations and aerial surveys. His special interest lies in the fossil record of the rhino.

Acknowledgements

It has been a privilege for us to communicate with you all and to personally meet and discuss many aspects of mutual interest in the compilation of this book. A subject as deep and emotional as the rhino has become requires careful consideration. We fully understand that there will be opinions that differ from our own point of view and we respect that.

Firstly, we wish to thank the contributors to this work: the late Jim Feely's family for permission to publish his paper, 'Black rhino, white rhino – what's in a name'; Lucky Mavrandonis and Sue Downey's chapter, 'A case study monitoring black rhino in SANParks'; Anton Walker co-author of *Rhino Keepers* for the chapters 'Rhino wars – guns and rhinos go together', 'Moving to save the rhino' and 'Living rhino in today's world'; and Yolan Friedmann of the Endangered Wildlife Trust and Dr John Hanks for their respective Afterwords.

We very much wanted to include a contribution by Prof. Jan Boeyens and Dr Maria van der Ryst, 'The cultural and symbolic significance of the African rhinoceros' (*Southern African Humanities* 26: 21–55, July 2014, KwaZulu-Natal Museum). This important review covers the traditional beliefs, perceptions and practices of argropastoralist societies in southern Africa in relation to the rhinoceros. Unfortunately, this was not possible due to space constraints. We know little about their past involvement and a greater awareness at some point will be valuable.

Our appreciation to the following people for comments on certain chapters: Dr George Hughes; Elise Maffue of 'StopRhinoPoaching' – there is little that does not escape her attention; Dr John Hanks who has been most helpful with suggestions and input; General Johan Jooste of SANParks; Pauline van der Spuy for facilitating a meeting with General Jooste; Pelham Jones, chairman of PROA who was always willing to provide information; Susie Offord-Woolley of SRI; Cathy Dean of SRI for permission to quote from their 'Fact File'; Yolan Friedmann of EWT; Lucy Vigne; and my son and co-author Anton Walker. My long-time friend Sally Antrobus is warmly thanked for her advice and for tackling the first editing of chapters 2 and 4.

We have been greatly assisted by the following colleagues who provided important information and discussion: Tony Conway of Ezemvelo Wildlife; Dr Michael Knight of AfRSG; Dr Richard Emsley of AfRSG; Michelle Pffab of SANBI; Professors M and A Saayman of North-West University; Erika Alberts of WRSA; Michael Eustace; John Raimondo; Dr Kelly Enright who wrote the Preface; Dr Kees Rookmarker;

OPPOSITE: Clive Walker in his bushveld studio with his fox terrier, Button, who had no fear of rhino. Photo: Bruno Zanzoterra.

Tessa Baber; Antoinette Ferriera; Dr Salmon Joubert; Karel Janse van Vuuren; Dr Jacques Flamand; Rael Loon; Dr Dave Cooper of Ezemvelo Wildlife; Chris Roche of Wilderness Safaris; Peter Anderson, a tourism property specialist; Dave Cooke for useful discussion; and my eldest son, Renning for IT input.

Our grateful thanks to a number of people who provided some truly outstanding photographic images: Michael Viljoen; George Hughes; Erica Alberts, editor of *Wildlife Ranching*; Catherina Hall-Martin for the photo taken by her late husband Anthony; Dana Allan of Wilderness Safaris; Susie Ellis of IRF; Deon de Villiers; Chris Serfontein; Brian Courtenay; Bruno Zanzottera; and Richard Wadley.

We should never overlook the role that our colleagues in the media play in bringing conservation issues to the wider world. It is been our good fortune over many years to work with many who we believe are the 'standard bearers' in this battle. We salute them all.

As always with any publication there is the publisher and staff, and we have been most fortunate over the past six years to work with Carol Broomhall of Jacana Media and her team: Carol is passionate about books and publishing and equally passionate about rhinos; Jenny Prangley, my editor, is thorough, patient and a real pleasure to work with, as are Nadia Goetham, Shawn Paikin, Megan Mance and Lara Jacob.

Our family are also ardent rhino lovers and we have all, Conita, Renning, Anton, Rene and myself, lived with rhinos for close on 35 years. What an incredible journey we have all shared together.

Every effort has been made to ensure the facts in this book are correct, and should we have omitted anyone in our acknowledgements, our sincere apologies for the oversight.

A publication of this nature would not be possible without the generous support of our sponsors who have enabled us to produce a work worthy of the 'rhinocerous', the landscapes and the people who daily put their lives on the line to ensure their survival. We are indeed grateful to Nicky and Strilli Oppenheimer, Duncan Parker and Gianni Ravazzotti. Worthy of mention as well is Duncan MacFadyen.